DAVID FERRY

The Georgics of Virgil

David Ferry, author of *Of No Country I Know: New and Selected Poems and Translations*, is the translator of *Gilgamesh* (1992); *The Odes of Horace* (1998); *The Eclogues of Virgil* (1999); and *The Epistles of Horace* (2001), winner of the Harold Morton Landon Translation Award—all published by FSG.

THE GEORGICS OF VIRGIL

THE

GEORGICS

OF VIRGIL

A TRANSLATION BY

DAVID FERRY

FARRAR, STRAUS AND GIROUX

NEW YORK

Farrar, Straus and Giroux
18 West 18th Street, New York 10011

Printed in the United States of America
Published in 2005 by Farrar, Straus and Giroux
First paperback edition, 2006

Some passages have previously appeared in AGNI, Arion, The Atlantic Monthly,
Kenyon Review, Literary Imagination, Persephone, Poetry, Raritan, The Threepenny
Review, and TriQuarterly.

Grateful acknowledgment is made for permission to reprint an excerpt from "The Farmer," by
William Carlos Williams, from Collected Poems: 1909–1939, Vol. I, copyright © 1938 by New
Directions Publishing Corp. Reprinted by permission of New Directions Publishing Corp.

Grateful acknowledgment is made to the publishers and the Trustees of the Loeb Classical Library
for permission to reprint Latin text from Virgil: Volume I—Eclogues, Georgics, Aeneid,
Books 1–6, Loeb Classical Library Volume 63, translated by H. R. Fairclough, revised by G. P.
Goold (Cambridge, Mass.: Harvard University Press, 1916); revision copyright © 1999 by the
President and Fellows of Harvard College. The Loeb Classical Library ® is a registered trademark
of the President and Fellows of Harvard College.

The Library of Congress has cataloged the hardcover edition as follows:
Virgil.
[Georgica. English & Latin]
The Georgics of Virgil : a translation / by David Ferry.— 1st ed.
p. cm.
A bilingual edition in English and Latin.
ISBN-13: 978-0-374-16139-2
ISBN-10: 0-374-16139-9 (hardcover : alk. paper)
1. Didactic poetry, Latin—Translations into English. 2. Agriculture—Poetry.
I. Ferry, David. II. Title.

PA6807.G4F4712 2005
872'.01—dc22

2004020023

Paperback ISBN-13: 978-0-374-53031-0
Paperback ISBN-10: 0-374-53031-9

Designed by Abby Kagan

www.fsgbooks.com

13 15 17 19 20 18 16 14

For Anne

You lie in our bed as if an orchard were over us.

You are what's fallen from those fatal boughs.

Where will we go, when they send us away from here?

Contents

Acknowledgments

The dedication page is the poem "In Eden," David Ferry, *Of No Country I Know: New and Selected Poems* (Chicago: University of Chicago Press, 1999), p. 127.

 I have consulted two other translations: that of H. Rushton Fairclough, revised by G. P. Goold, Loeb Classical Library (Cambridge, Mass.: Harvard University Press, 1999), and the great seventeenth-century translation by John Dryden, which I read in *The Poetical Works of John Dryden*, ed. George R. Noyes (Boston: Houghton Mifflin, 1950). I am extremely indebted to the commentaries of Richard Thomas, *Virgil: Georgics*, 2 vols. (Cambridge: Cambridge University Press, 1988); R.A.B. Mynors, *Virgil: Georgics* (Oxford: Clarendon Press, 1990); and for the Glossary, to J. E. Zimmerman, *Dictionary of Classical Mythology* (New York: Harper and Row, 1964). And of course I have consulted a number of commentaries, among them *The Cambridge Companion to Virgil* (Cambridge: Cambridge University Press, 1997), especially the articles by William Batstone, R. J. Tarrant, and Charles Martindale; also L. P. Wilkinson, *The Georgics of Virgil: A Critical Survey*, and A. J. Boyle, *The Chaonian Dove: Studies in the Eclogues, Georgics, and Aeneid of Virgil* (Leiden: E. J. Brill, 1986); Monica R. Gale, *Virgil on the Nature of Things* (New York: Cambridge University Press, 2000); Jasper Griffin, *Virgil* (New York: Oxford University Press, 1986); Nicholas Horsfall, ed., *A Companion to the Study of Virgil* (Leiden: E. J. Brill, 1995); M. Owen Lee, *Virgil as Orpheus: A Study of the Georgics* (Albany, N.Y.: Albany State University Press, 1996); Ramsay MacMullen, *Changes in the Roman Empire: Essays in the Ordinary* (Princeton, N.J.: Princeton University Press, 1990), *Corruption and the Decline of Rome* (New Haven, Conn.: Yale University Press, 1988), and *Romanization in the Time of Augustus* (New Haven, Conn.: Yale University Press, 2000); Gary B. Miles, *Virgil's Georgics: A New Interpretation* (Berkeley: University of California Press, 1980); Christine Perkell, *The Poet's Truth: A Study of the Poet in Virgil's Georgics* (Berkeley: University of California Press, 1989); Ronald Syme, *The Roman Revolution* (Oxford: Clarendon Press,

1939); Michael Putnam, *Virgil's Poem of the Earth* (Princeton, N.J.: Princeton University Press, 1979); Richard Thomas, *Lands and Peoples in Roman Poetry: The Ethnographical Tradition* (Cambridge: Cambridge Philological Society, 1982), and *Reading Virgil and His Texts* (Ann Arbor: Michigan University Press, 1999).

It would be absurd to try to list the names of all the friends—scholars, poets, and fellow translators—who have generously helped me out, the list would be so long.

I'm very grateful to the staff of Farrar, Straus and Giroux, especially Annie Wedekind, James Wilson, Abby Kagan, and Susan Goldfarb.

Most of all, I'm indebted to Jonathan Galassi, to Richard Thomas, and, as always, to Anne Ferry.

This book is also dedicated to the cottage industry, David, Elizabeth, and Stephen; and to Isaiah and Sebastian.

Introduction

In order for men to know what might be coming,
Drought, or torrential rain, winds bringing the cold,
Jove, the father himself, provided signs:
The warnings of the moon in its monthly round;
What it might mean when the wind suddenly dies;
What the farmer sees, and sees again, that tells him
To keep his cattle close to the barn and shelter.
Just when the wind of an impending storm
Begins to blow, perhaps in the inlet channel
There are signs of swelling and heaving in the water,
Or maybe, far away, in the high mountains,
A sudden loud crash is heard, or the murmur of trees
In the neighboring wood all of a sudden sounds different.
Then too the sea-swells rise against the keels,
And the gulls fly landward crying in their flight,
And the little sea coots run along the shore,
Looking as if they're frolicking as they go,
And the heron deserts its own familiar marsh
To get up as high as it can, over the clouds.

And the passage continues, telling you about how, when the storm is coming on, "[y]ou'll see a star precipitously falling, / Trailing its shining wake along the blackness," and "bits of straw and leaves toss on the wind / And feathers float and play upon the waters," and "you can see the cranes depart / For the deep inland valleys," and crying swallows will fly "[a]round and around the pools in their excitement," and the heifer "looks up at the sky" and "sniffs the change in the air," and "even indoors, at night, / The young girl at her spinning sees the signs / Of what it is that's going to happen soon: / The oil in the lighted lamp sputters and sparks; / There's a buildup of putrid fungus on the wick."

The cadence begins with human beings for whom Jupiter has provided signs, and it ends with the young woman reading the signs of the coming storm in the buildup of putrid fungus on the candlewick. But she herself is a sign of what's coming, and so are the sea coots running along the shore, and the crashing sound in the mountains, and the sudden swelling of seas, and all the other creatures and phenomena of the world. They are all creatures together, all readers of signs, and signs themselves, and all of them are going to suffer the storm's coming on. It is a nature in which wine no longer flows in the streams, for when Jupiter overthrew his father Saturn the whole world changed:

> It was Jupiter who put the deadly poison
> Into the fangs of serpents; commanded the wolf
> To seek and find its prey; ordained that the storm
> Should cause the sea to rise and flood the land;
> Stripped from the leaves of oaks the dewlike honey
> That made them glisten there; hid fire from man;
> Turned off the flow of wine that everywhere
> Ran in the streams . . .

In Virgil's great myth of the fall of man, it is not through man's own fault, as in the Judeo-Christian myth, but simply because this is how things are, and are going to be, for all creatures, the hills and seas, the fields, the grain, the vines, the beasts and birds, the bees, and the creature man himself.

Everywhere in the four books of the poem there are ecstatic and tender celebrations of the very life in things: "The trees that rise up of their own free will / Into the light, wild, happy in the strength / They got from nature's power in the earth"; the cucumber tendril that "winds and turns and coils / Its way through the grass"; the promising colt who's "a higher stepper than all the other / Foals there are in the fields, and puts his feet / More lightly down again on the soft turf"; the "murmuring humming" of the bees as "[t]hey groom themselves and hither and thither flit / Around the doors and thresholds of their houses"; and the ravens whose hoarse voice you can hear, "repeated maybe / Three or four times over," or, high in the trees, "talking together, / In some uncanny way expressing delight / At being home and safe in their sweet nests / Along with their young." And this joy in the very life of things is always, one way or another, coupled with a darker sense.

It is a fallen world and all creatures are vulnerable. The beautiful high-stepping horse grows old and sick: "[T]he horse that was once / Victorious now miserably sinks . . . / Over and over again pounding the earth / With a disconsolate hoof . . ." The bees fall ill and you can see "[t]he sick ones not yet dead that hang almost / Motionless around the doors outside, / With crossed and tangled feet . . ." The vulnerability of these creatures and what they do, and what happens to them, is essential to the beauty and value the poem sees in them. Pity is the context for the poem's celebrations; admiration is the context for the poem's commiserations.

It is remarkable how in this great work the triumphs and sufferings of the creatures other than man are fully meaningful and substantiated in themselves; they're never merely background for, nor merely metaphors for, the story of men. The dignity of what they are is never exploited as pathetic fallacy; there is no condescension in the poem toward those others who share our fallen world with us. The respect and admiration Virgil has for the little goats, who are "able / To forage in woods and on the Lycaean heights, / Feeding on brambles and mountain-loving briar," and who know how "to come home all by themselves / With their kids following after, the she-goats' udders / So full that they can scarcely clear the threshold," is not unlike the respect and admiration he has for the old Corycian man, triumphantly gathering for supper what he'd managed to grow "[o]n a little patch of land that nobody wanted, / Too poor for oxen to plow, unfit for pasture, / Not right for planting vines."

But if the *Georgics* is a poem about all vulnerable creatures, it is also of course a poem by a human being with his own vital human interests, and the whole truth and intention of the poem is not only what all the creatures of Jupiter's fallen world share together, but the special meaning of this situation for man. Jupiter "[s]tripped from the leaves of oaks the dewlike honey / That made them glisten there; hid fire from man; / Turned off the flow of wine that everywhere / Ran in the streams; all this so want should be / The cause of human ingenuity, / And ingenuity the cause of arts." Jupiter ordained that "the way should not be easy." He first "established the art of cultivation, / Sharpening with their cares the skills of men, / Forbidding the world he rules to slumber in ease." So human culture began. Little by little, men learned to plow, learned to make fire and traps for hunting, lines and nets for fishing; they learned to count the stars and give them names. "Then followed other arts; and everything / Was toil, relentless toil, urged on by need," the need for it never exhausted: "three times a year, / Four times, you must turn the soil, to open it up . . . / The farmer's labor circles back on him / As the seasons of the year roll back around / To where they were and walk in their own footsteps."

The poem is one of the great songs, maybe the greatest we have, of human accomplishment in the difficult circumstances of the way things are. You can hear in the poem the pleasure it takes, how proud it feels about what men know, learning how to bring about their precarious successes. There's the man who "induces water to flow down from a brook / Through channels toward his planting, and when there's drought / And the field is parched and scorched and the little plants / Look like they may be dying, behold, there's water." There's "a farmer I know of [who] sits up till all hours / In front of the fire in winter intently using / His knife to fashion torches out of branches. / Meanwhile his wife is doing winter chores, / Singing a song to solace her as she works." There's joy in Virgil's description of the minutiae of tasks well done, testing the soil, for example, by taking a wicker basket down from the roof-tree where it was hanging: "[P]our in / Fresh water from the spring; you'll see the water / Make its way through, and the big drops fall into / The receptacle below; then taste the water; / The taste will tell the story." Or teaching your bullocks to begin to get used to the yoke: "And after a little while, their free necks having / Become accustomed to their servitude, / Tie the young bullocks together two by two, / Collar tethered to collar, and make them learn / To walk together, step by step, a pair."

"The farmer works the soil with his curved plow; / This is the work he does, and it sustains / His country, and his family, and his cattle, / His worthy bullocks and his herd of cows. / No rest from this." But his successes are indeed only precarious, and the failures are inevitable. A river floods, and Acerrae in the Campania is emptied of its people. A shepherd is careless with his fire: a spark "catches under the bark of an olive tree, / And burns at first unnoticed there, and then / Takes hold of the trunk, flows up to the leaves above, / And sending a huge roar up into the sky, / Then rages conquering, victorious . . ." Sometimes catastrophe comes down upon the grain:

I remember the times when I have seen a farmer
Lead his laborers into the yellow fields
To gather the ears of barley when they're ready
To be stripped from their brittle stalks, and all of a sudden,
The warring winds came down and tore up the plants
By their very roots and carried them aloft
And swept them all away, light stalk and stubble,
Flying off somewhere on the black whirlwind,
The whole promising crop, lock, stock, and barrel.

Much worse has happened and will happen again. There was a plague and all the animals died: "Pale Tisiphone rages . . . and heaps up in the stables / Disgusting rotting deliquescent bodies," and "men had to scratch at the earth by themselves with harrows, / And use their own fingernails to dig the holes / To plant their seeds in, and their own strained necks / To drag their creaking wagons up the hills." And because men in Jupiter's disposition of things are vulnerable not only to weather and plague but to their own natures, there is warfare, brother against brother, threatening to bring down Rome, *rerum facta est pulcherrima*, "the most beautiful thing there is":

> *O Caesar . . .*
> *Right and wrong are turned into one another;*
> *War everywhere in the world; crimes everywhere,*
> *In every way and every shape and form;*
> *No honor at all is given to the plow;*
> *The fields are barren and empty, the farmers gone;*
> *The crooked sickles are beaten into swords . . .*
> *. . . Mars rages everywhere.*

Virgil wrote the poem during the 30s B.C.E., completing it in 29, just as the civil war between Octavian and Antony had come to a climax and an end; this passage reflects Virgil's fears and anxieties born of his memories of this civil war and those that came before, "[a]ll the blood shed that to this day's unpaid for."

Over and over it is as if it all had to be started again. *Labor omnia vicit / improbus, et duris urgens in rebus egestas*: "[A]nd everything / Was toil, relentless toil, urged on by need." Culture, in the fallen world of Jupiter, is always near the fragile beginnings of its making and always near its potential end. Existence itself is fragile in this world, and the more loved because it is so, having to be so carefully and anxiously constructed and maintained by toil and ingenuity and arts. Maybe Virgil was so interested in the skills of agriculture and animal husbandry and viniculture and beekeeping because he came from people who worked at such things, and also because they're beautiful and touching and interesting in themselves. But it also has to be because these ingenuities and arts, still with us and still essential, are always, though present, still back there at the beginning, when we fell and nature became imperfect, and culture had to be constructed. Human culture is always so present, and so past, and its future always so uncertain. The poem is haunted by its earliness and lateness. The *Georgics* is the fundamental poem.

The other creatures in their own ways and degrees have their cultures, and their own awareness of who and what they are, their own pride, their own loves, their wars, the accomplishments and failures of their labors. But men are unlike the other creatures in having the obligation of learning to know most fully what their labor is, how it succeeds and fails, and in having the obligation of knowing how to sing about it. The *Georgics* is a fulfillment of that obligation. And in the end, just like the *Eclogues*, it acknowledges the limitations of what song can do. Orpheus, the greatest singer, out of his very love of Eurydice, vulnerable to his own nature, must lose her as he turns back to her, and cannot retrieve her from oblivion:

> *And a sudden madness seized him, madness of love,*
> *A madness to be forgiven if Hell but knew*
> *How to forgive; he stopped in his tracks, and then,*
> *Just as they were just about to emerge*
> *Out into the light, suddenly, seized by love,*
> *Bewildered into heedlessness, alas!*
> . . .
> *His purpose overcome, he turned, and looked*
> *Back at Eurydice! And then and there*
> *His labor was spilled and flowed away like water.*
>
> *Disintegrating into air, she was*
> *Dispersed away and vanished from his eyes*
> *And never saw him again, and he was left*
> *Clutching at shadows, with so much still to say.*

When John Dryden finished his translation of the *Georgics* at the end of the seventeenth century, he called Virgil's poem "the best poem by the best poet."

Virgil says, in the Second Georgic, that he is undertaking to "sing Hesiod's song in Roman towns," and certainly the *Works and Days* of the ancient Greek writer are one of his models in his accounts of the days and works of the Italian farmer. But the *Georgics'* complex relations to other sources, ancient Greek and Hellenistic and Roman, Homer and Callimachus and Lucretius, Aristus and Cato and Varro and Gallus, are far beyond my competence to describe independently. There is a clear and instructive account in Richard F. Thomas's edition and commentary, *Virgil's Georgics*, published in 1988 by the Cambridge

University Press. Nor do I presume to give a comprehensive account of how the presence of the *Georgics* is felt in the poetry of our own language.

Of course there are marvelous instances in Milton's poetry of the particular verbal presence of Virgil's poem—in "Lycidas," for example:

> *What could the Muse herself that Orpheus bore,*
> *The Muse herself, for her enchanting son,*
> *Whom Universal nature did lament,*
> *When by the rout that made the hideous roar,*
> *His gory visage down the stream was sent,*
> *Down the swift Hebrus to the Lesbian shore.*

But it isn't, in the case of Milton, a matter of verbal echoes merely. The presence of the *Georgics* in one's reading of *Paradise Lost*, and of *Paradise Lost* in one's reading of the *Georgics*, is powerfully felt throughout because these poems are our two great original responses to our common human knowledge, already expressed in the prior mythologies of Genesis and the stories of the Greeks—that we and the nature we inhabit are fallen, and that we must somehow bravely deal with this: "In the sweat of thy face shalt thou eat bread, till thou return unto the ground." Grant all the differences between the *Georgics* and *Paradise Lost*: it is still true that the two great poems read one another.

The *Georgics* is always there in what might be called the pastoral of hard work, in Spenser, in songs in Shakespeare's plays, in Ben Jonson's "To Penshurst," for example, and in seventeenth-century lyric poems by many writers. There are many eighteenth-century poems, written often for gentlemen farmers or for readers imagining themselves to be so, which are consciously "georgic" in being, or pretending to be, manuals for the technology of farmwork and production. There is James Thomson's grand poem, based in many ways on the *Georgics*, "The Seasons"; and at the end of the eighteenth century, the poems of George Crabbe and William Blake. John Keats's "To Autumn" is a deeply georgic poem. Most deeply of all, perhaps, there is the poetry of Wordsworth, especially in those passages (in *The Prelude*, in "Michael," in "The Ruined Cottage," in many other poems) where admiration and pity for the incessant labors of men are linked with anxiety about the vulnerability of the culture that labor constructs, "urged on by need." Wordsworth in *The Prelude* speaks of a little mountain community and says, in lines where pity and admiration are one and the same:

> *. . . Immense*
> *Is the recess, the circumambient world*
> *Magnificent, by which they are embraced.*
> *They move about upon the soft green turf:*
> *How little they, they and their doings seem,*
> *Their herds and flocks about them, they themselves,*
> *And all that they can further or obstruct!*
> *Through utter weakness pitiably dear*
> *As tender Infants are; and yet how great!*

The voice we hear is Virgilian and georgic. In these respects the poetry of Robert Frost, whom Helen Bacon has called "the most georgic of poets," is the heir of the georgic Wordsworth, in such poems as Frost's great "Directive": "Weep for what little things could make them glad," and "The Strong Are Saying Nothing": "Men work alone, their lots plowed far apart, / One stringing a chain of seed in an open crease, / And another stumbling after a halting cart."

But the *Georgics* is such an essential account that one reads through its eyes even great texts where, so far as I know, no specific source-relationship exists or where such specificity is not the point. For example, Whitman's ecstatic catalogues, full of admiration and pity for the labors of men and their vulnerability to circumstance, are "georgic" because the *Georgics* helps one to experience their power. It is just so when one reads William Carlos Williams's poem "The Farmer":

> *The farmer in deep thought*
> *is pacing through the rain*
> *among his blank fields, with*
> *hands in pockets,*
> *in his head*
> *the harvest already planted.*
> *A cold wind ruffles the water*
> *among the browned weeds.*
> *On all sides*
> *the world rolls coldly away:*
> *black orchards*
> *darkened by the March clouds—*
> *leaving room for thought.*
> *Down past the brushwood*
> *bristling by*
> *the rainsluiced wagonroad*

looms the artist figure of
the farmer—composing—
antagonist

Virgil (Publius Vergilius Maro) was born near the town of Mantua, Italy, in 70 B.C.E. His father was probably a landowner, and it is said that his farm was appropriated when the ruler Octavian (Caesar Augustus) distributed lands to his returning soldiers after the battle of Philippi. Virgil studied in Cremona and then Milan and finally in Rome, where he was ultimately sponsored by Maecenas, who was also the patron of the poet Horace; thus Virgil and Horace belonged to the literary circle around Octavian.

Virgil's *Bucolics*, which we know as the *Eclogues*, are his earliest authenticated work, dating at the latest from the mid-30s B.C.E., and the *Georgics* were said to have been read to Octavian in 29. Virgil began the writing of his epic of the founding of Rome, the *Aeneid*, shortly afterward, and had almost completed it when, attempting to return to Rome after three years in Greece and Asia Minor, he fell ill. He died at the port Brundisium in September, 19 B.C.E., and was buried near Naples, where he owned a villa, his principal residence.

He had left instructions that his unfinished *Aeneid* be burned, but Augustus ordered his literary executors, Varius Rufus and Plotius Tucca, to preserve it and publish it. It was issued two years later.

A NOTE ON THE TRANSLATION

In translating the *Georgics* I have used iambic pentameter, with frequent anapestic substitutions, as my metrical system. In English a six-foot line comparable to Virgil's hexameters would, in my opinion, be impossible to manage without extreme artificiality.

In the case of many Latin words (proper names, names of places, and so forth), I have sometimes barbed the vowel sound to indicate the metrical stress, and sometimes to indicate that a final *e* is to be heard as pronounced, not silent. For example I have used a stress-mark in the name "Cyréné" over the second syllable and over the final *e*.

Let me echo a statement I have made in connection with my other translations from the Latin. I have tried to be as faithful as possible. English is of course not Latin and I am most certainly not Virgil. Every act of translation is an act of interpretation, and every choice of English word or phrase, every placement of those words or phrases in sentences—made in obedience to the laws and habits of English, not Latin, grammar, syntax, and idioms—and every metrical decision—made in obedience to English, not Latin, metrical laws and habits—reinforces the differences between the interpretation and the original. This is true however earnestly the interpretation aims to represent the sense of Virgil's *Georgics*, the effects and implications of his figures of speech, the controlled variety and passion of his tones of voice. It is my hope that this translation, granting such differences between English and Latin, is reasonably close.

FIRST GEORGIC

Quid faciat laetas segetes, quo sidere terram
vertere, Maecenas, ulmisque adiungere vites
conveniat, quae cura boum, qui cultus habendo
sit pecori, apibus quanta experientia parcis,
hinc canere incipiam. vos, o clarissima mundi
lumina, labentem caelo quae ducitis annum;
Liber et alma Ceres, vestro si munere tellus
Chaoniam pingui glandem mutavit arista,
poculaque inventis Acheloia miscuit uvis;
et vos, agrestum praesentia numina, Fauni
(ferte simul Faunique pedem Dryadesque puellae!):
munera vestra cano. tuque o, cui prima frementem
fudit equum magno tellus percussa tridenti,
Neptune; et cultor nemorum, cui pinguia Ceae
ter centum nivei tondent dumeta iuvenci;
ipse, nemus linquens patrium saltusque Lycaei,
Pan, ovium custos, tua si tibi Maenala curae,
adsis, o Tegeaee, favens, oleaeque Minerva
inventrix, uncique puer monstrator aratri,
et teneram ab radice ferens, Silvane, cupressum;
dique deaeque omnes, studium quibus arva tueri,
quique novas alitis non ullo semine fruges,

What's right for bringing abundance to the fields;
Under what sign the plowing ought to begin,
Or the marrying of the grapevines to their elms;
How to take care of the cattle and see to their breeding;
Knowing the proper way to foster the bees
As they go about their work; Maecénas, here
Begins my song. You brightest lights of the sky
That shepherd the year as it moves along its way;
O Liber, O generous Ceres, if by your favor
The earth exchanged the acorns fallen from oak trees
For ripening ears of grain, and blent the newly-
Discovered grape with the waters of Achelóus;
And you, O Fauns, you presences of the fields
(O Fauns and Dryads, come and dance together!),
I sing to praise the blessings of your gifts.
And you, O Neptune, you whose mighty trident
Struck the earth and the nickering steed was born;
You, guardian of the groves, because of whom
Three hundred snow-white cattle peacefully browse
The rich Ceáean glades; and you, O Pan,
The keeper of the flocks, consent to come
From your Lycáean woods and thickets and
From Máenalus that you love; Minerva, you,
Inventrix of the olive; and Triptólemus,
Who taught us how to use the crooked plow;
And you, Sylvanus, carrying in your hand
A cypress tree uprooted from the ground;
You gods and goddesses all, who with such kindness
Watch over our fields and vineyards and who nurture

quique satis largum caelo demittitis imbrem.
tuque adeo, quem mox quae sint habitura deorum
concilia incertum est, urbesne invisere, Caesar,
terrarumque velis curam, et te maximus orbis
auctorem frugum tempestatumque potentem
accipiat, cingens materna tempora myrto;
an deus immensi venias maris ac tua nautae
numina sola colant, tibi serviat ultima Thule,
teque sibi generum Tethys emat omnibus undis;
anne novum tardis sidus te mensibus addas,
qua locus Erigonen inter Chelasque sequentis
panditur (ipse tibi iam bracchia contrahit ardens
Scorpios et caeli iusta plus parte reliquit):
quidquid eris (nam te nec sperant Tartara regem
nec tibi regnandi veniat tam dira cupido,
quamvis Elysios miretur Graecia campos
nec repetita sequi curet Proserpina matrem),
da facilem cursum atque audacibus adnue coeptis,
ignarosque viae mecum miseratus agrestis
ingredere et votis iam nunc adsuesce vocari.

    Vere novo, gelidus canis cum montibus umor
liquitur et Zephyro putris se glaeba resolvit,
depresso incipiat iam tum mihi taurus aratro
ingemere, et sulco attritus splendescere vomer.

The fruits that seed themselves without our labor,
And all the crops, with rain that falls from heaven;
And you, O Caesar, although we know not yet
What place among the councils of the gods
Will be your place, whether you choose to be
The guardian supervisor of our cities,
Caretaker of our lands, your temples bound
With the myrtle wreath of Venus your goddess mother,
So that the whole great world acknowledges you
The author of our bounty and lord of seasons,
Or whether you come as god of the immense
Unmeasurable sea, the god all sailors
Pray to, the god that Ultima Thule swears
Subjection to, and Tethys offers her waves
As dower for your marriage to her daughter,
Or whether you'll appear in the autumn sky,
A new zodiacal star in the place between
The Virgin and where Scorpio will retract
His claws to make a place in the heavens for you—
Whatever it be (the Underworld would not
Dare hope for you as ruler, and may the dread
Desire of kingship there never be yours—
Though Greece fell under the spell of Elysian Fields
And Proserpina when her mother called her home
Was reluctant to return to the fields above),
Grant me the right to enter upon this bold
Adventure of mine, grant that I make it through,
Pitying me along with those farmers who need
To be taught to find their way, and grant that we
May come into your presence with our prayers.

When spring begins and the ice-locked streams begin
To flow down from the snowy hills above
And the clods begin to crumble in the breeze,
The time has come for my groaning ox to drag
My heavy plow across the fields, so that
The plow blade shines as the furrow rubs against it.

illa seges demum votis respondet avari
agricolae, bis quae solem, bis frigora sensit;
illius immensae ruperunt horrea messes.
ac prius ignotum ferro quam scindimus aequor,
ventos et varium caeli praediscere morem
cura sit ac patrios cultusque habitusque locorum,
et quid quaeque ferat regio et quid quaeque recuset.
hic segetes, illic veniunt felicius uvae,
arborei fetus alibi, atque iniussa virescunt
gramina. nonne vides, croceos ut Tmolus odores,
India mittit ebur, molles sua tura Sabaei,
at Chalybes nudi ferrum, virosaque Pontus
castorea, Eliadum palmas Epiros equarum?
continuo has leges aeternaque foedera certis
imposuit natura locis, quo tempore primum
Deucalion vacuum lapides iactavit in orbem,
unde homines nati, durum genus. ergo age, terrae
pingue solum primis extemplo a mensibus anni
fortes invertant tauri, glaebasque iacentis
pulverulenta coquat maturis solibus aestas;
at si non fuerit tellus fecunda, sub ipsum
Arcturum tenui sat erit suspendere sulco:
illic, officiant laetis ne frugibus herbae,
hic, sterilem exiguus ne deserat umor harenam.

Not till the earth has been twice plowed, so twice
Exposed to sun and twice to coolness will
It yield what the farmer prays for; then will the barn
Be full to bursting with the gathered grain.
And yet, if the field's unknown and new to us,
Before our plow breaks open the soil at all,
It's necessary to study the ways of the winds
And the changing ways of the skies, and also to know
The history of the planting in that ground,
What crops will prosper there and what will not.
In one place grain grows best, in another, vines;
Another's good for the cultivation of trees;
In still another the grain turns green unbidden.
From Lydian Timólus, don't you see,
Our fragrant saffron comes, from India
Our ivory, from soft Arabia
Our frankincense, our iron ore from the naked
Chalýbian tribes, from Pontus castor oil
From the testicles of beavers, and from Epírus
The mares that are the mothers of the horses
That are born to win Olympic victories.
Nature apportioned it thus to diverse places;
So it has been from the very beginning of time,
When Deucalion threw the stones into the empty
Landscape and thus created stony men.
So, if the soil of the field you're getting ready
Is rich and fertile, set your oxen to work
In early spring to turn the earth, and then
Let it lie waiting for summer's heat to bake it,
So as to keep the weeds from flourishing
And interfering with the joyous grain;
But if the soil is sandy, leave it alone;
In early September it will be enough,
Just as Arctúrus rises in the sky,
To rake it lightly, trying to keep what little
Moisture that may be there from drying out.
And every second season let the land
Be idly fallow, so that what happens happens;
Or, under a different constellation, sow

Alternis idem tonsas cessare novalis
et segnem patiere situ durescere campum;
aut ibi flava seres mutato sidere farra,
unde prius laetum siliqua quassante legumen
aut tenuis fetus viciae tristisque lupini
sustuleris fragilis calamos silvamque sonantem.
urit enim lini campum seges, urit avenae,
urunt Lethaeo perfusa papavera somno:
sed tamen alternis facilis labor, arida tantum
ne saturare fimo pingui pudeat sola neve
effetos cinerem immundum iactare per agros.
sic quoque mutatis requiescunt fetibus arva,
nec nulla interea est inaratae gratia terrae.
saepe etiam steriles incendere profuit agros
atque levem stipulam crepitantibus urere flammis;
sive inde occultas vires et pabula terrae
pinguia concipiunt, sive illis omne per ignem
excoquitur vitium atque exsudat inutilis umor,
seu pluris calor ille vias et caeca relaxat
spiramenta, novas veniat qua sucus in herbas,
seu durat magis et venas adstringit hiantis,
ne tenues pluviae rapidive potentia solis
acrior aut Boreae penetrabile frigus adurat.
   Multum adeo, rastris glaebas qui frangit inertis
vimineasque trahit crates, iuvat arva, neque illum
flava Ceres alto nequiquam spectat Olympo;
et qui, proscisso quae suscitat aequore terga,
rursus in obliquum verso perrumpit aratro
exercetque frequens tellurem atque imperat arvis.
   Umida solstitia atque hiemes orate serenas,
agricolae: hiberno laetissima pulvere farra,

The seeds for a crop of yellow barley, having
Uprooted and carried away the wild pulse with
Its quivering pods shaking with laughter, or
The pods of the slender vetch, or the rattling stalks
Of the lupine plant. Flax scorches the earth; oats too;
And poppies suffused all through with the sleep of Lethe.

By alternating crops you make toil easy.
And don't be ashamed to saturate the soil
With the rich dung of beasts, and scatter the sooty
Ashes left from your household fires last winter.
Changing the crops is restful for the fields;
Sometimes they're not ungrateful not to be plowed;
They need to rest. Sometimes it's a good idea
To torch the empty fields and let the flames
Burn the stubble away: maybe the earth
Thus takes into itself rich nourishment
And secret power, or it may be that the heat
Bakes away taints in the soil, or that it gets rid
Of undesirable moisture by sweating it out;
Or that it opens up new avenues
And hidden passages by which the juice
Will make its way to the new young leaves that need it;
Or, on the contrary, maybe it narrows the veins
And hardens the earth around them, affording them
Protection from the violent pelting rain
Or from the heat of the sun, or winter cold.

And in addition the farmer does well for the land
Who uses his hoe to break up the clotted glebes
And drags the wicker harrow over them;
Not without cause does golden Ceres look
Benignly down upon him from the height
Of Mount Olympus. And he does well who drives
His plow obliquely crosswise back across
The ridges that he raised when he plowed before
And breaks them down. It's thus he disciplines
And trains the soil he works, and gives it order.
Farmers, pray for summers with lots of rain,

laetus ager; nullo tantum se Mysia cultu
iactat et ipsa suas mirantur Gargara messes.
quid dicam, iacto qui semine comminus arva
insequitur cumulosque ruit male pinguis harenae,
deinde satis fluvium inducit rivosque sequentis
et, cum exustus ager morientibus aestuat herbis,
ecce supercilio clivosi tramitis undam
elicit? illa cadens raucum per levia murmur
saxa ciet, scatebrisque arentia temperat arva.
quid qui, ne gravidis procumbat culmus aristis,
luxuriem segetum tenera depascit in herba,
cum primum sulcos aequant sata, quique paludis
collectum umorem bibula deducit harena?
praesertim incertis si mensibus amnis abundans
exit et obducto late tenet omnia limo,
unde cavae tepido sudant umore lacunae.

    Nec tamen, haec cum sint hominumque boumque labores
versando terram experti, nihil improbus anser
Strymoniaeque grues et amaris intiba fibris
officiunt aut umbra nocet. pater ipse colendi
haud facilem esse viam voluit, primusque per artem
movit agros, curis acuens mortalia corda,
nec torpere gravi passus sua regna veterno.
ante Iovem nulli subigebant arva coloni:
ne signare quidem aut partiri limite campum
fas erat; in medium quaerebant, ipsaque tellus
omnia liberius nullo poscente ferebat.

And winters with lots of sun; the grain is pleased,
The fields are pleased, when the soil is dry in winter.
Thus Mýsia and Gárgara, exultant,
Will glory in the harvests that come in.

How shall I tell of the man who flings down the seeds,
And then attacks the field, lays low and levels
The heaped-up sandy soil that gets in the way
And induces water to flow down from a brook
Through channels toward his planting, and when there's drought
And the field is parched and scorched and the little plants
Look like they may be dying, behold, there's water?
You can hear the muttering guttural sound of the water
Moving down through the smooth stones of the channels
And gushing into the fields to quench their thirst.
And how shall I tell of the man who, when the stalks
Are on the verge of being overburdened
By the weight of the growing ears, summons his sheep
To graze the ebullient plant back down to where
The tender leaves and the furrow's top are equal?
Or the man who uses sand to drink up water
Collected in marshy places when a river
Overflows, and the lowland hollows steam?

🐦

But though both men and cattle do their work,
And do it well, there are the mischievous geese
And Strymonian cranes, and choking fibrous weeds,
And overshading trees, to trouble the crops.
For Father Jupiter himself ordained
That the way should not be easy. It was he
Who first established the art of cultivation,
Sharpening with their cares the skills of men,
Forbidding the world he rules to slumber in ease.
Before Jove's time no farmer plowed the earth;
It was forbidden to mark out field from field,
Setting out limits, one from another; men shared
All things together and Earth quite freely yielded

ille malum virus serpentibus addidit atris,
praedarique lupos iussit pontumque moveri,
mellaque decussit foliis, ignemque removit,
et passim rivis currentia vina repressit,
ut varias usus meditando extunderet artes
paulatim, et sulcis frumenti quaereret herbam,
ut silicis venis abstrusum excuderet ignem.
tunc alnos primum fluvii sensere cavatas;
navita tum stellis numeros et nomina fecit,
Pleïades, Hyadas, claramque Lycaonis Arcton;
tum laqueis captare feras et fallere visco
inventum et magnos canibus circumdare saltus;
atque alius latum funda iam verberat amnem
alta petens, pelagoque alius trahit umida lina;
tum ferri rigor atque argutae lammina serrae
(nam primi cuneis scindebant fissile lignum),
tum variae venere artes. labor omnia vicit
improbus, et duris urgens in rebus egestas.

Prima Ceres ferro mortalis vertere terram
instituit, cum iam glandes atque arbuta sacrae
deficerent silvae et victum Dodona negaret.
mox et frumentis labor additus, ut mala culmos
esset robigo segnisque horreret in arvis
carduus; intereunt segetes, subit aspera silva,
lappaeque tribolique, interque nitentia culta

The gifts of herself she gave, being unasked.
It was Jupiter who put the deadly poison
Into the fangs of serpents; commanded the wolf
To seek and find its prey; ordained that the storm
Should cause the sea to rise and flood the land;
Stripped from the leaves of oaks the dewlike honey
That made them glisten there; hid fire from man;
Turned off the flow of wine that everywhere
Ran in the streams; all this so want should be
The cause of human ingenuity,
And ingenuity the cause of arts,
Finding little by little the way to plant
New crops by means of plowing, and strike the spark
To ignite the hidden fire in veins of flint.
Then rivers began to sense that hollow canoes
Were floating upon their waters; sailors began
To count the stars in the sky and give them names:
Pleiades, Hýades, Arctos, starry child
Of Lycaón. And then they learned to snare
Wild beasts in traps and fool song birds with lime;
Here one man lashes the river with his line,
Seeking the depths; and there another drags
His dripping fishnet through the ocean waters.
Then came the hardness of iron and then the shriek
Of the sharp blade of the saw as it made its way
(For earlier men used wedges to cleave their wood);
Then followed other arts; and everything
Was toil, relentless toil, urged on by need.

There came a day when in the sacred wood
The acorns and arbutus began to fail
And the oracle of Zeus denied men food.
It was then that Ceres first taught how to turn
The soil with iron instruments, as trouble
Came to the grain, the evil rust-blight eating
Into the stems, the sluggish hairy thistle
Prospering in the fields, destroying crops,
And in their place a thorny undergrowth,
Caltrops, goose grass, and other burry things.

infelix lolium et steriles dominantur avenae.
quod nisi et adsiduis herbam insectabere rastris
et sonitu terrebis aves et ruris opaci
falce premes umbras votisque vocaveris imbrem,
heu magnum alterius frustra spectabis acervum
concussaque famem in silvis solabere quercu.

Dicendum et quae sint duris agrestibus arma,
quis sine nec potuere seri nec surgere messes:
vomis et inflexi primum grave robur aratri,
tardaque Eleusinae matris volventia plaustra,
tribulaque traheaeque et iniquo pondere rastri;
virgea praeterea Celei vilisque supellex,
arbuteae crates et mystica vannus Iacchi.
omnia quae multo ante memor provisa repones,
si te digna manet divini gloria ruris.
continuo in silvis magna vi flexa domatur
in burim et curvi formam accipit ulmus aratri.
huic a stirpe pedes temo protentus in octo,
binae aures, duplici aptantur dentalia dorso.
caeditur et tilia ante iugo levis altaque fagus
stivaque, quae currus a tergo torqueat imos,
et suspensa focis explorat robora fumus.

Possum multa tibi veterum praecepta referre,
ni refugis tenuisque piget cognoscere curas.

Among the smiling cultivated plants
Darnel and tares and sterile oat-grass thrive.
Therefore unless you take up your hoe, attacking
The enemy weeds over and over again,
And over and over again shout at the birds
To scare them away, and use your pruning knife
To keep on cutting back the overgrowth
That threatens your plants with shade, you will, alas,
End up, defeated, staring at your neighbor's
Granary full of corn, and in the woods
You'll shake the oak tree, frantic for something to eat.

Next I must tell about the weapons the farmer
Needs for sowing his seeds and raising his crops:
The plow blade in the curved plow's wooden frame,
Ceres' lumbering wagon, the heavy carts
And the heavy threshing-sledge, the ponderous hoes,
The wicker hurdles and all the other tools
That Céleus of Eleúsis thought of,
And Íacchus's mystic winnowing-basket.
You have to have all these for when you need them,
If you want to win the glory the land can offer.
A young elm in the woods is bent by the force
Of the will of muscle to make the beam or stock
That takes the curving shape of the plow they're making.
To the end of this is attached an eight-foot pole,
Fitted with "ears" that shape and mold the earth
As the plowing proceeds, and a double crosspiece that functions
So as to be a socket for the share.
Then, too, in the woods, a little linden tree
Is felled to make the yoke, and a beech for the handle
With which to steer and turn the chariot plow.
But before they can be used, the linden wood
And beech wood must be cured by hearth-fire smoke.
I could tell you many old sayings and many maxims
(Unless you're unwilling to hear such trivial things).

area cum primis ingenti aequanda cylindro
et vertenda manu et creta solidanda tenaci,
ne subeant herbae neu pulvere victa fatiscat,
tum variae inludant pestes: saepe exiguus mus
sub terris posuitque domos atque horrea fecit,
aut oculis capti fodere cubilia talpae,
inventusque cavis bufo et quae plurima terrae
monstra ferunt, populatque ingentem farris acervum
curculio atque inopi metuens formica senectae.
    Contemplator item, cum se nux plurima silvis
induet in florem et ramos curvabit olentis:
si superant fetus, pariter frumenta sequentur,
magnaque cum magno veniet tritura calore;
at si luxuria foliorum exuberat umbra,
nequiquam pinguis palea teret area culmos.
semina vidi equidem multos medicare serentis
et nitro prius et nigra perfundere amurca,
grandior ut fetus siliquis fallacibus esset,
et, quamvis igni exiguo, properata maderent.
vidi lecta diu et multo spectata labore
degenerare tamen, ni vis humana quotannis
maxima quaeque manu legeret. sic omnia fatis
in peius ruere ac retro sublapsa referri,

First, you have to level the threshing ground
With a heavy stone roller, and after that, with your hands
You must bind the soil together with sticky clay
So it becomes solidified and makes
A kind of floor. This is to keep the weeds
From coming up from under, and keep the soil
From drying out and crumbling into dust,
Opening holes for pests to get up through
And make a fool of you. The little mouse
Builds his house and storehouse under the ground.
The mole, down there, digs sightlessly through the earth
To make his chambers. Toads are found in holes,
And many other monsters the earth begets.
The weevil can ravage almost all your grain,
And ants are ravagers too, fearful of being
Poverty-stricken when they get to be old.

Consider this too: if in the woods the almond
Lavishly blooms so that her boughs bend low,
Fragrant with blossom, then too the crops will be
Lavishly rich as well, with the great heat
Of the great exultant threshing following on;
But if the tree be overburdened with leaves
And therefore over-copiously shady,
The frustrated thresher will thrash and beat the stalks
And chaff will be the only riches they yield.
Many's the time when I myself have seen
The farmer treating seedpods with the black
Oil of olive lees, or else with nitre,
Then simmer them over a gentle fire, trying
To soften the deceitful husks and make them
Yield more fully than they otherwise might.
I have seen seeds, no matter how carefully
Selected and with many pains examined
To be the best, degenerate nevertheless,
Unless, year in, year out, over and over,
Men labor to find the largest seeds again.
All things by nature are ready to get worse,
Lapse backward, fall away from what they were,

non aliter quam qui adverso vix flumine lembum
remigiis subigit, si bracchia forte remisit,
atque illum in praeceps prono rapit alveus amni.

    Praeterea tam sunt Arcturi sidera nobis
Haedorumque dies servandi et lucidus Anguis,
quam quibus in patriam ventosa per aequora vectis
Pontus et ostriferi fauces temptantur Abydi.
Libra die somnique pares ubi fecerit horas
et medium luci atque umbris iam dividit orbem,
exercete, viri, tauros, serite hordea campis
usque sub extremum brumae intractabilis imbrem;
nec non et lini segetem et Cereale papaver
tempus humo tegere et iamdudum incumbere aratris,
dum sicca tellure licet, dum nubila pendent.
vere fabis satio; tum te quoque, Medica, putres
accipiunt sulci et milio venit annua cura,
candidus auratis aperit cum cornibus annum
Taurus et adverso cedens Canis occidit astro.
at si triticeam in messem robustaque farra
exercebis humum solisque instabis aristis,
ante tibi Eoae Atlantides abscondantur
Cnosiaque ardentis decedat stella Coronae,
debita quam sulcis committas semina quamque
invitae properes anni spem credere terrae.
multi ante occasum Maiae coepere; sed illos
exspectata seges vanis elusit avenis.
si vero viciamque seres vilemque phaselum,

Just as if one who struggles to row his little
Boat upstream against a powerful current
Should but for a moment relax his arms, the current
Would carry him headlong back again downstream.

And furthermore we must observe the stars
And where they are and at what time of year,
Arctúrus, and the Goats, and the bright Snake Star,
Just as the sailor must, when making for home,
Braving the stormy seas past Pontus coast,
And Abýdos, at the jaws of the Hellespont.
From the time of the autumnal equinox
When light and shade divide the world between them,
And sleep and waking are equal, oxen and men
Must set themselves to work, planting the barley,
Until the time when the rains are about to come,
And winter the intractable begins.
Autumn is also the time to plant your flax
And Ceres' poppy seed, and not too late
For bending over the plow, while the earth is dry
And the clouds still high, the rains still holding off.
Spring is the season for planting beans, and the time
When the loosened furrows will accept the clover,
And the millet newly planted every year,
As snow-white Taurus with his golden horns
Comes up in the springtime sky and Canis falls,
Yielding his annual place to his opposite star.
But if it's a crop of wheat, or maybe spelt,
Or corn you're tilling the ground for, wait to plant
The intended seeds in the furrows that you've plowed,
Entrusting your yearly hope to the grudging earth
Till the Pleiades take their leave of the morning sky
And till you no longer can see the bright stars shine
In the crown of Ariadne. Many have sowed
Before the departure of Maia, and they have found
That the crop they expected has fooled them with empty husks.
But if you're not above the wish to plant

nec Pelusiacae curam aspernabere lentis,
haud obscura cadens mittet tibi signa Bootes;
incipe et ad medias sementem extende pruinas.

    Idcirco certis dimensum partibus orbem
per duodena regit mundi sol aureus astra.
quinque tenent caelum zonae: quarum una corusco
semper sole rubens et torrida semper ab igni;
quam circum extremae dextra laevaque trahuntur
caeruleae, glacie concretae atque imbribus atris;
has inter mediamque duae mortalibus aegris
munere concessae divum, et via secta per ambas,
obliquus qua se signorum verteret ordo.
mundus, ut ad Scythiam Riphaeasque arduus arces
consurgit, premitur Libyae devexus in Austros.
hic vertex nobis semper sublimis; at illum
sub pedibus Styx atra videt Manesque profundi.
maximus hic flexu sinuoso elabitur Anguis
circum perque duas in morem fluminis Arctos,
Arctos Oceani metuentes aequore tingui.
illic, ut perhibent, aut intempesta silet nox,
semper et obtenta densentur nocte tenebrae;
aut redit a nobis Aurora diemque reducit,
nosque ubi primus equis Oriens adflavit anhelis,
illic sera rubens accendit lumina Vesper.
hinc tempestates dubio praediscere caelo
possumus, hinc messisque diem tempusque serendi,

Vetch, or kidney beans, or Egyptian lentils,
Boötes as it sets will send no signs
Prohibitive to this; you may plant them then,
Or any time before the winter's frosts.

To govern all this and give it order, the sun
Traverses the fixed divisions of the heavens,
Making his golden journey through all twelve
Zodiacal constellations of the skies.
Five zones partition the universe of things.
One glows for ever with the scorching heat
And flashing light for ever of the sun;
To the right and left, at the farthest extremes of the world,
Two zones of ice and stormy dark for ever;
Between these two and the central sunlit zone
Are two the gods allow to mortal men,
And between these two a heavenly ellipsis
In which the turning signs may be observed.
To the north our world steeply ascends to the high
Riphaean cliffs of Scythia, and then
To the south sinks down to the sands of the Libyan desert.
One pole is always high above our heads;
The other is far far down below our feet—
Only black Styx and the Shades of the Dead can see it.
There in that sky the constellation Snake
Slides forth and slithers its riverine coils around
And in between the Bears that fear the water
And never descend to feel cold Ocean's touch;
Down there, they say, there is unchanging darkness,
And endless silence, there, is everywhere.
Or else, they say, the Dawn returns down there,
Bringing them back the light of our previous day;
Or when we feel the breath of the morning sun,
Brought back to us by his panting horses, then
Vesper, down there, is shining in their sky.

Thus, though the sky is changeful, men can predict
The seasons as they change and what they bring:
The time for harvest, the time for planting seeds,

et quando infidum remis impellere marmor
conveniat, quando armatas deducere classis,
aut tempestivam silvis evertere pinum.
nec frustra signorum obitus speculamur et ortus,
temporibusque parem diversis quattuor annum.

Frigidus agricolam si quando continet imber,
multa, forent quae mox caelo properanda sereno,
maturare datur: durum procudit arator
vomeris obtunsi dentem, cavat arbore lintres,
aut pecori signum aut numeros impressit acervis.
exacuunt alii vallos furcasque bicornis
atque Amerina parant lentae retinacula viti.
nunc facilis rubea texatur fiscina virga,
nunc torrete igni fruges, nunc frangite saxo.
quippe etiam festis quaedam exercere diebus
fas et iura sinunt: rivos deducere nulla
religio vetuit, segeti praetendere saepem,
insidias avibus moliri, incendere vepres,
balantumque gregem fluvio mersare salubri.
saepe oleo tardi costas agitator aselli
vilibus aut onerat pomis, lapidemque revertens
incusum aut atrae massam picis urbe reportat.

Ipsa dies alios alio dedit ordine Luna
felicis operum. quintam fuge: pallidus Orcus
Eumenidesque satae; tum partu Terra nefando

The time to brave the unfaithful sea with oars,
The time to bring the warboats down to the water,
The time to fell the pines with which to build them.
It's not without reason that we've learned to watch
The rising and the setting of the stars,
Marking the equal seasons as they change.

When the cold rains come and they have to stay indoors,
The laborers are able to get things done
That in better weather they'd have to hurry to do:
One hammering on the share where it was blunted;
Another hollowing branches, making wine troughs;
Others are sorting out and labeling
The heaps of garnered grain; branding the beasts;
Sharpening stakes and two-pronged forks; or making
Willow-shoot ties to bind up sagging vines;
Weaving new baskets, using pliant twigs;
Roasting corn on the fire of the household oven,
Or on the hearthstone grinding it into meal.
There are many tasks that are right and proper to do,
No matter whether or not it's a holiday.
There's no observance that says you're not permitted
To irrigate your plantings or put in a hedge
For their protection, or lay down snares for birds,
Set fire to brambles, or bring your baaing flock
Down to the stream to give them a healthy bath.
Sometimes, on such days, too, a farmer will load
His donkey's sides with bargain fruit, or oil,
And drive the recalcitrant beast to town to market,
And come back home with pitch he'd traded for,
Or a new millstone to use to grind his grain.

Luna has so commanded that there are days
That are right for doing certain kinds of work
And days that are wrong. Avoid the fifth of the month,
The day pale Orcus and the Eumenides
Were born, and with horrible labor Earth brought forth

Coeumque Iapetumque creat saevumque Typhoea
et coniuratos caelum rescindere fratres.
ter sunt conati imponere Pelio Ossam
scilicet, atque Ossae frondosum involvere Olympum;
ter pater exstructos disiecit fulmine montis.
septima post decimam felix et ponere vitem
et prensos domitare boves et licia telae
addere. nona fugae melior, contraria furtis.
    Multa adeo gelida melius se nocte dedere,
aut cum sole novo terras inrorat Eous.
nocte leves melius stipulae, nocte arida prata
tondentur, noctes lentus non deficit umor.
et quidam seros hiberni ad luminis ignes
pervigilat ferroque faces inspicat acuto;
interea longum cantu solata laborem
arguto coniunx percurrit pectine telas,
aut dulcis musti Volcano decoquit umorem
et foliis undam trepidi despumat aëni.
at rubicunda Ceres medio succiditur aestu,
et medio tostas aestu terit area fruges.
nudus ara, sere nudus; hiems ignava colono.
frigoribus parto agricolae plerumque fruuntur
mutuaque inter se laeti convivia curant.
invitat genialis hiems curasque resolvit,
ceu pressae cum iam portum tetigere carinae,
puppibus et laeti nautae imposuere coronas.

Raging Typhoeus, and Iápetus, and Coeus,
And the Giant Brothers, they who conspired together
To bring down Heaven. Three times on Pelion
They piled Mount Ossa and on Ossa piled
Leafy Olympus. Three times the lightning bolt
Of Father Jupiter was hurled, and split
The mountains apart and spoiled the Giants' plot.
The seventeenth is good for planting vines,
Breaking in oxen, preparing the loom for weaving.
The full moon on the ninth is good for those
Like runaways, who need to find their way,
And bad for thieves, who need not to be seen.

There are many tasks it's better to perform
In the very early morning, just at sunrise,
When the dew is everywhere, or in the night,
When it's certain to be cool. Nighttime is good
For mowing the dry meadows or shearing the stubble;
The moisture makes it easier then to do so.
A farmer I know of sits up till all hours
In front of the fire in winter intently using
His knife to fashion torches out of branches.
Meanwhile his wife is doing winter chores,
Singing a song to solace her as she works,
Running the shrilling shuttle through the web,
Or boiling down the sweet must on the fire,
Or using leaves to skim the overflowing
Foam of the liquid in the bubbling pot.
The heat of summer noon is best for cutting
Ceres' golden grain and threshing it.
Work naked in the fields in the heat of summer,
Plowing the earth and scattering in the seeds.
Wintertime's the time for idleness.
Cold weather's when the laborers can rest
And feast together on what they'd labored for:
The winter festiveness unravels cares—
It's as when a ship at last comes into port
With a full cargo, the voyage finally over,
And the joyful crew bedecks the decks with garlands.

sed tamen et quernas glandes tum stringere tempus
et lauri bacas oleamque cruentaque myrta,
tum gruibus pedicas et retia ponere cervis
auritosque sequi lepores, tum figere dammas
stuppea torquentem Balearis verbera fundae,
cum nix alta iacet, glaciem cum flumina trudunt.
    Quid tempestates autumni et sidera dicam,
atque, ubi iam breviorque dies et mollior aestas,
quae vigilanda viris, vel cum ruit imbriferum ver,
spicea iam campis cum messis inhorruit et cum
frumenta in viridi stipula lactentia turgent?
saepe ego, cum flavis messorem induceret arvis
agricola et fragili iam stringeret hordea culmo,
omnia ventorum concurrere proelia vidi,
quae gravidam late segetem ab radicibus imis
sublimem expulsam eruerent; ita turbine nigro
verrit hiems culmumque levem stipulasque volantis.
saepe etiam immensum caelo venit agmen aquarum
et foedam glomerant tempestatem imbribus atris
collectae ex alto nubes; ruit arduus aether,
et pluvia ingenti sata laeta boumque labores
diluit; implentur fossae et cava flumina crescunt

But winter's also the time for gathering acorns
For mast to feed the beasts, and for gathering berries
Of blood-red myrtle and laurel to scent the wine;
And the time for pressing olives for their oil;
For hunting long-eared hares; putting down snares,
Traps for the unsuspecting legs of cranes;
Setting out nets that the stags get entangled in;
Whirling the Baleáric hempen slingshots
To stun and kill the does, while the snow is deep
And ice accumulates on the frozen rivers.

How shall I tell of autumn and its changes
And its changing constellations as the days
Grow shorter than they were, and summer's heat
Grows less than it had been? How shall I tell
Of all the things the farmers must watch out for?
Of spring and springtime rains down-pouring on
The fields of bearded greening stalks of grain,
Its young ears swelling with their milky juice?
I remember the times when I have seen a farmer
Lead his laborers into the yellow fields
To gather the ears of barley when they're ready
To be stripped from their brittle stalks, and all of a sudden
The warring winds came down and tore up the plants
By their very roots and carried them aloft
And swept them all away, light stalk and stubble,
Flying off somewhere on the black whirlwind,
The whole promising crop, lock, stock, and barrel.
Sometimes, too, there advances in the sky
A tremendous congregated mass of waters
Gathered from the topmost reach of the heavens
Into a hideous tempest of black clouds;
Then suddenly this wall of sky falls down
Upon the earth, and all its flooding water
Washes away the joyous crops and all
The work that men and oxen did together.
The dikes flood over; the roaring rivers and

cum sonitu fervetque fretis spirantibus aequor.
ipse pater media nimborum in nocte corusca
fulmina molitur dextra: quo maxima motu
terra tremit; fugere ferae et mortalia corda
per gentes humilis stravit pavor: ille flagranti
aut Atho aut Rhodopen aut alta Ceraunia telo
deicit; ingeminant Austri et densissimus imber,
nunc nemora ingenti vento, nunc litora plangunt.
hoc metuens caeli menses et sidera serva,
frigida Saturni sese quo stella receptet,
quos ignis caelo Cyllenius erret in orbis.
in primis venerare deos, atque annua magnae
sacra refer Cereri laetis operatus in herbis
extremae sub casum hiemis, iam vere sereno.
tum pingues agni et tum mollissima vina,
tum somni dulces densaeque in montibus umbrae.
cuncta tibi Cererem pubes agrestis adoret:
cui tu lacte favos et miti dilue Baccho,
terque novas circum felix eat hostia fruges,
omnis quam chorus et socii comitentur ovantes,
et Cererem clamore vocent in tecta; neque ante
falcem maturis quisquam supponat aristis,
quam Cereri torta redimitus tempora quercu
det motus incompositos et carmina dicat.

The spuming inlets seethe and overflow;
The steaming ocean waters rock and heave.
When Jupiter himself in the midnight storm
Hurls down his thunderbolts from his right hand,
The shocked world shakes, the wild beasts run away,
And all men cower in terror everywhere;
Mountains collapse under his terrible strokes,
Acroceraunia, Rhodope, or Athos;
The winds and the rain redouble and redouble;
The woods and the sea cliffs wail under the storm.

Fearing such things, pay heed to the months and stars
And what they have to tell you: where in the sky
Saturn's cold star retires to; where in the sky
The wandering fires of Mercury can be seen,
And at what time of the year. Above all else,
Be sure to pay due reverence to the gods.
When spring has come and winter is over and done with,
Yield to great Ceres the yearly rite you owe her.
Spring is the season when the lambs are plump,
The season when the wine is mellowest,
The time of year when sleep is sweetest of all,
And the shadows on the hills are at their softest.
See to it that your laborers all take part
In the rituals of the worship of the goddess:
Let the offering of honeycombs be washed
With milk and with soft wine; lead the propitious
Sacrificial victim thrice around
The fields the sacrifice is for, while all
The laborers follow along, joyfully shouting,
Calling on Ceres to come in under their roofs;
Let none of them use his sickle to cut a single
Ear of the ripened grain before he has wreathed
His brow with an oak-leaf garland and danced his artless
Dance and sung his song in honor of Ceres.

Atque haec ut certis possemus discere signis,
aestusque pluviasque et agentis frigora ventos,
ipse pater statuit, quid menstrua luna moneret,
quo signo caderent Austri, quid saepe videntes
agricolae propius stabulis armenta tenerent.
continuo ventis surgentibus aut freta ponti
incipiunt agitata tumescere et aridus altis
montibus audiri fragor, aut resonantia longe
litora misceri et nemorum increbrescere murmur.
iam sibi tum a curvis male temperat unda carinis,
cum medio celeres revolant ex aequore mergi
clamoremque ferunt ad litora, cumque marinae
in sicco ludunt fulicae, notasque paludes
deserit atque altam supra volat ardea nubem.
saepe etiam stellas vento impendente videbis
praecipites caelo labi, noctisque per umbram
flammarum longos a tergo albescere tractus;
saepe levem paleam et frondes volitare caducas,
aut summa nantis in aqua colludere plumas.
at Boreae de parte trucis cum fulminat et cum
Eurique Zephyrique tonat domus, omnia plenis
rura natant fossis atque omnis navita ponto
umida vela legit. numquam imprudentibus imber
obfuit: aut illum surgentem vallibus imis
aëriae fugere grues, aut bucula caelum
suspiciens patulis captavit naribus auras,
aut arguta lacus circumvolitavit hirundo
et veterem in limo ranae cecinere querelam.
saepius et tectis penetralibus extulit ova
angustum formica terens iter, et bibit ingens

In order for men to know what might be coming,
Drought, or torrential rain, winds bringing the cold,
Jove, the father himself, provided signs:
The warnings of the moon in its monthly round;
What it might mean when the wind suddenly dies;
What the farmer sees, and sees again, that tells him
To keep his cattle close to the barn and shelter.
Just when the wind of an impending storm
Begins to blow, perhaps in the inlet channel
There are signs of swelling and heaving in the water,
Strange echoing noises in the coastal cliffs,
Or maybe, far away, in the high mountains,
A sudden loud crash is heard, or the murmur of trees
In the neighboring wood all of a sudden sounds different.
Then too the sea-swells rise against the keels,
And the gulls fly landward crying in their flight,
And the little sea coots run along the shore,
Looking as if they're frolicking as they go,
And the heron deserts its own familiar marsh
To get up as high as it can, above the clouds.
Sometimes, too, when the storm is coming on,
You'll see a star precipitously falling,
Trailing its shining wake along the blackness;
Light bits of straw and leaves toss on the wind
And feathers float and play upon the waters.
But when there's lightning in the northern sky
Or thunder where the East or West Winds come from,
Then all the fields and ditches will be flooded,
And out at sea in all the boats the sailors
Will gather in their dripping sails in fear.
No storm comes on without giving you any warning.
High in the sky you can see the cranes depart
For the deep inland valleys; in the field the heifer
Looks up at the sky and sniffs the change in the air
With open nostrils; the crying swallows fly
Around and around the pools in their excitement;
The old frogs in the mud croak out the song
Of their ancient grievances; the busy ant
Runs anxiously back and forth on her little path,

arcus, et e pastu decedens agmine magno
corvorum increpuit densis exercitus alis.
iam varias pelagi volucres et quae Asia circum
dulcibus in stagnis rimantur prata Caystri,
certatim largos umeris infundere rores,
nunc caput obiectare fretis, nunc currere in undas
et studio incassum videas gestire lavandi.
tum cornix plena pluviam vocat improba voce
et sola in sicca secum spatiatur harena.
ne nocturna quidem carpentes pensa puellae
nescivere hiemem, testa cum ardente viderent
scintillare oleum et putris concrescere fungos.

    Nec minus ex imbri soles et aperta serena
prospicere et certis poteris cognoscere signis:
nam neque tum stellis acies obtunsa videtur
nec fratris radiis obnoxia surgere Luna,
tenuia nec lanae per caelum vellera ferri;
non tepidum ad solem pinnas in litore pandunt
dilectae Thetidi alcyones, non ore solutos
immundi meminere sues iactare maniplos.
at nebulae magis ima petunt campoque recumbunt,
solis et occasum servans de culmine summo
nequiquam seros exercet noctua cantus.

Bringing her eggs out from the innermost cells
Of her underground house; an enormous rainbow drinks
From the waters of the earth; an army of rooks
Rises in full formation, and flies away
With a clatter of wings, leaving the pasture behind;
All kinds of sea birds, too, like those who play
And search about for what they can find in the standing
Pools and meadows near an Asian river—
You can see how they compete with one another,
Dipping their heads, and shaking the copious
Water-drops over their shoulders, racing each other
In and out of the waves, aimlessly
Intent on having the pleasure of taking a bath;
And then the ill-natured crow walks by himself
Along the beach, and with his harsh loud voice
Invokes the rain. And even indoors, at night,
The young girl at her spinning sees the signs
Of what it is that's going to happen soon:
The oil in the lighted lamp sputters and sparks;
There's a buildup of putrid fungus on the wick.

After the rain goes by you can expect
A period of bright sun and cloudless sky
And there are many signs foretelling this:
The edges of the lights of the stars at night
Are sharply defined, and Luna when she rises
Shines with a light so clear it seems it must
Be all her own, unborrowed from her brother's;
No mackerel clouds foretelling rain are seen;
No halcyon birds, the favorites of Thetis,
Are seen on shore, opening wide their wings
To catch the warmth of the sun; nor will you see
The filthy pigs in the barnyard using their snouts
To toss their straw uneasily about.
At such a time the mists find out the lowest
Places that they can to spread upon,
And as from some high place the gloomy owl

apparet liquido sublimis in aëre Nisus
et pro purpureo poenas dat Scylla capillo:
quacumque illa levem fugiens secat aethera pinnis,
ecce inimicus, atrox, magno stridore per auras
insequitur Nisus; qua se fert Nisus ad auras,
illa levem fugiens raptim secat aethera pinnis.
tum liquidas corvi presso ter gutture voces
aut quater ingeminant, et saepe cubilibus altis
nescio qua praeter solitum dulcedine laeti
inter se in foliis strepitant; iuvat imbribus actis
progeniem parvam dulcisque revisere nidos.
haud equidem credo, quia sit divinitus illis
ingenium aut rerum Fato prudentia maior;
verum ubi tempestas et caeli mobilis umor
mutavere vias et Iuppiter uvidus Austris
denset erant quae rara modo, et quae densa relaxat,
vertuntur species animorum, et pectora motus
nunc alios, alios dum nubila ventus agebat,
concipiunt: hinc ille avium concentus in agris
et laetae pecudes et ovantes gutture corvi.
   Si vero solem ad rapidum lunasque sequentis
ordine respicies, numquam te crastina fallet
hora, neque insidiis noctis capiere serenae.
luna revertentis cum primum colligit ignis,
si nigrum obscuro comprenderit aëra cornu,
maximus agricolis pelagoque parabitur imber:
at si virgineum suffuderit ore ruborem,
ventus erit; vento semper rubet aurea Phoebe.
sin ortu quarto (namque is certissimus auctor)

Watches the sun go down, her boding song
Is purposeless and void. Then Nisus the hawk
High in the cloudless evening sky pursues
His daughter Scylla to take revenge on her
For her theft of his lock of hair, that lost his city;
She flees through the evening air on her little wings;
Wherever she goes her father follows after,
Implacable, frightful, his wings loudly whirring;
And she flees through the evening air on her little wings,
And wherever she goes her father follows after.
Quieter than it usually is, the hoarse
Voice of the raven is heard, repeated maybe
Three or four times over, or, high in the trees,
Among the leaves, you can hear them talking together,
In some uncanny way expressing delight
At being home and safe in their sweet nests
Along with their young. I do not think this means
That they've been granted wisdom by the gods
Or a special providential power by Fate;
But when in its changing ways the weather changes
And Jupiter Plúvius causes the rain to fall,
Then causes the skies to clear, then something changes,
Changes in their minds, something is different,
Different in their breasts from what it was
When the wind was bringing clouds and bringing rain.
That's why the birds are singing, and why the lambs
Look happy in the fields, and the ravens are talking.

Pay attention to the sun and moon as they
Follow on one another in their order:
Tomorrow will be true to what you saw,
Nor will a cloudless night betray your hopes.
As soon as the moon collects her fires and rises,
If there's a dark mist drifting across her horns,
Then farmers and sailors know a storm is coming;
And if her face is glowing, faintly rosy,
As if she were blushing, there will be windy weather;

pura neque obtunsis per caelum cornibus ibit,
totus et ille dies et qui nascentur ab illo
exactum ad mensem pluvia ventisque carebunt,
votaque servati solvent in litore nautae
Glauco et Panopeae et Inoo Melicertae.

Sol quoque et exoriens et cum se condet in undas
signa dabit; solem certissima signa sequentur,
et quae mane refert et quae surgentibus astris.
ille ubi nascentem maculis variaverit ortum
conditus in nubem medioque refugerit orbe,
suspecti tibi sint imbres; namque urget ab alto
arboribusque satisque Notus pecorique sinister.
aut ubi sub lucem densa inter nubila sese
diversi rumpent radii, aut ubi pallida surget
Tithoni croceum linquens Aurora cubile,
heu! male tum mitis defendet pampinus uvas:
tam multa in tectis crepitans salit horrida grando.
hoc etiam, emenso cum iam decedit Olympo,
profuerit meminisse magis; nam saepe videmus
ipsius in vultu varios errare colores:
caeruleus pluviam denuntiat, igneus Euros;
sin maculae incipiunt rutilo immiscerier igni,
omnia tum pariter vento nimbisque videbis
fervere. non illa quisquam me nocte per altum
ire neque a terra moneat convellere funem.

But if, on the fourth day of the month, her light
Is perfectly clear as she moves across the sky
And her horns are not at all obscured, that day
And all the offspring of that day until
The end of the month will be free from wind and rain,
And sailors, having safely come back home,
Will pay their vows, on shore, in gratitude
To Melicérta, and Glaucus, and Panopéa.

Whether it's when he first comes into view,
Or plunges out of sight beneath the waves,
The sun will give us signs; signs we can follow,
Indisputable signs, that follow upon him,
At dawn or when the stars begin to come out.
If in the morning the clouds hide him away
Or if his light is only fitfully seen,
In random patches faintly marking the ground,
Or if his disk looks shrunken behind the mist,
Better prepare for rain: the South Wind's coming,
The enemy of trees and herds and crops,
Bearing down on the land from out at sea.
But if the shafts of sunlight burst, this way
And that way, violently through the thick
Clouds that cover the sky, or if the Dawn
Is pale as she arises and departs
From Tithónus's saffron couch, oh, then, there'll be
Little the vine leaves will be able to do
To keep the ripening grapes from coming to harm,
As battering hailstones rattle on all the roofs.
And in the evening, when having crossed the sky,
The sun descends from the heavens, taking his leave,
These are the signs that men may profit from:
Often at evening we see how various colors
Wander across the face of the setting sun,
And each tells a different story about the future—
Dark blue means rain; red means wind is coming;
But blotches of dark and blotches of glowing fire
Mean that the world will boil and seethe with storm.
On such a night let nobody try to persuade me

at si, cum referetque diem condetque relatum,
lucidus orbis erit, frustra terrebere nimbis
et claro silvas cernes Aquilone moveri.

Denique, quid vesper serus vehat, unde serenas
ventus agat nubes, quid cogitet umidus Auster,
sol tibi signa dabit. solem quis dicere falsum
audeat? ille etiam caecos instare tumultus
saepe monet fraudemque et operta tumescere bella.
ille etiam exstincto miseratus Caesare Romam,
cum caput obscura nitidum ferrugine texit
impiaque aeternam timuerunt saecula noctem.
tempore quamquam illo tellus quoque et aequora ponti,
obscenaeque canes importunaeque volucres
signa dabant. quotiens Cyclopum effervere in agros
vidimus undantem ruptis fornacibus Aetnam,
flammarumque globos liquefactaque volvere saxa!
armorum sonitum toto Germania caelo
audiit, insolitis tremuerunt motibus Alpes.
vox quoque per lucos vulgo exaudita silentis
ingens, et simulacra modis pallentia miris
visa sub obscurum noctis, pecudesque locutae,
infandum! sistunt amnes terraeque dehiscunt,
et maestum inlacrimat templis ebur aeraque sudant.
proluit insano contorquens vertice silvas
fluviorum rex Eridanus camposque per omnis
cum stabulis armenta tulit. nec tempore eodem
tristibus aut extis fibrae apparere minaces

To go out onto the deep or to unloose
The rope that keeps me tied up to the land.
But if, either when he brings back the day
Or when he returns the day into the night,
His face is perfectly clear, then you need have
No fear at all that there will be bad weather;
You'll see the woods sway peacefully in the breeze.

The sun gives signs, telling you from what region
The wind is to come that blows away the clouds
Or what the stormy south is thinking of—
And who dares doubt his word? For, many times
The sun has warned us of dark events to come,
Treachery, deceit, clandestine plots, and war.
When Caesar's light was quenched, the shining face
Of the sun, in pity for Rome, was covered with darkness,
And that impious generation was in fear
That there would thenceforth be eternal night.
And not only the sun but the earth and the sea gave signs,
And dogs and birds gave signs, of ill to come.
How many times have we seen Aetna burst,
Sending forth rocks and whirling balls of flame,
Pouring her rivers of fire down on the plains.
Germany heard across the skies the sound
Of warfare, and the Alps themselves were shaken.
At twilight, in the evening, ghosts were seen,
Or strange pale simulacra of human beings;
In a silent grove—many attested to this—
A loud voice was suddenly heard to speak;
And animals, too, were suddenly heard to speak—
Unspeakable!—with voices of men and women.
Rivers stopped in their courses; earth opened up wide;
Tears dropped from the eyes of ivory statues in temples;
Bronzes broke into sweat; the river Po,
The king of rivers, insanely overflowed
And with its whirling waters washed away
Entire uprooted forests and carried off
Whole herds and their stables together across the plains.
At this time too, menacing threads showed up

aut puteis manare cruor cessavit, et altae
per noctem resonare lupis ululantibus urbes.
non alias caelo ceciderunt plura sereno
fulgura nec diri totiens arsere cometae.
ergo inter sese paribus concurrere telis
Romanas acies iterum videre Philippi;
nec fuit indignum superis, bis sanguine nostro
Emathiam et latos Haemi pinguescere campos.
scilicet et tempus veniet, cum finibus illis
agricola incurvo terram molitus aratro
exesa inveniet scabra robigine pila,
aut gravibus rastris galeas pulsabit inanis,
grandiaque effossis mirabitur ossa sepulcris.

    Di patrii, Indigetes, et Romule Vestaque mater,
quae Tuscum Tiberim et Romana Palatia servas,
hunc saltem everso iuvenem succurrere saeclo
ne prohibete! satis iam pridem sanguine nostro
Laomedonteae luimus periuria Troiae;
iam pridem nobis caeli te regia, Caesar,
invidet atque hominum queritur curare triumphos;
quippe ubi fas versum atque nefas: tot bella per orbem,
tam multae scelerum facies; non ullus aratro
dignus honos, squalent abductis arva colonis,
et curvae rigidum falces conflantur in ensem.
hinc movet Euphrates, illinc Germania bellum;
vicinae ruptis inter se legibus urbes
arma ferunt; saevit toto Mars impius orbe:

In the entrails of birds the frightened priests interpret;
And blood was in the water drawn up from wells;
The ululating howls of wolves were heard
Echoing in the streets of high hill-towns.
Never were there more times when lightning struck
Down from a perfectly cloudless sky; and never
Were there more terrible comets to be seen.

Therefore a second time Philippi saw
Armies of brother Romans using Roman
Weapons to clash in war with one another,
And the gods above decided it was not
Unfitting that the Macedonian fields
Should be nourished with our blood a second time,
And someday, in those fields the crooked plow
Of a farmer laboring there will turn up a spear,
Almost eaten away with rust, or his heavy hoe
Will bump against an empty helmet, and
He'll wonder at the giant bones in that graveyard.

You gods and heroes of my native country,
You, Romulus, you, mother Vesta, who
Protect the Tiber and the Palatine Hill,
At least do not prohibit this young prince
From coming to the rescue of this people
In their distress; our blood has paid enough
For Priam's father's broken promise at Troy;
O Caesar, the gods begrudge your care for us;
Right and wrong are turned into one another;
War everywhere in the world; crimes everywhere,
In every way and every shape and form;
No honor at all is given to the plow;
The fields are barren and empty, the farmers gone;
The crooked sickles are beaten into swords;
There's war on the Euphrates; on the Rhine;
Neighboring cities break their mutual oaths,
Sword against sword; Mars rages everywhere.

ut cum carceribus sese effudere quadrigae,
addunt in spatia, et frustra retinacula tendens
fertur equis auriga neque audit currus habenas.

It's as when from the starting line at the track
The chariots break loose. Lap after lap,
Around and around, and the driver pulls on the reins
And it's no use, and the chariot rushes on,
All out of control . . .

SECOND GEORGIC

Hactenus arvorum cultus et sidera caeli:
nunc te, Bacche, canam, nec non silvestria tecum
virgulta et prolem tarde crescentis olivae.
huc, pater o Lenaee (tuis hic omnia plena
muneribus, tibi pampineo gravidus autumno
floret ager, spumat plenis vindemia labris),
huc, pater o Lenaee, veni nudataque musto
tingue novo mecum dereptis crura cothurnis.
    Principio arboribus varia est natura creandis.
namque aliae nullis hominum cogentibus ipsae
sponte sua veniunt camposque et flumina late
curva tenent, ut molle siler lentaeque genistae,
populus et glauca canentia fronde salicta;
pars autem posito surgunt de semine, ut altae
castaneae, nemorumque Iovi quae maxima frondet
aesculus, atque habitae Grais oracula quercus.
pullulat ab radice aliis densissima silva,
ut cerasis ulmisque; etiam Parnasia laurus
parva sub ingenti matris se subicit umbra.

So far my song has been about the stars
And about the cultivation of the fields;
And Bacchus, now my song will be of you,
And the young new growth of saplings in the woods
And the offspring of slow-growing olive trees.
O Bacchus, come, be here amid your plenty;
The field, with all the produce of the vines,
Is flourishing for you, and the foaming wine
Is almost overflowing in the vats.
Come, Bacchus, tread barefoot and buskinless,
As I do, in the must the wine is made from.

Nature has many ways of growing trees.
Some kinds spring up and spread all by themselves,
As if they came from nowhere, and they take
Possession of the fields and all along
The banks of winding streams: the yielding osier,
The pliant broom, the poplar, and the throngs
Of willows with their gray-green-silvery leaves.
Some, like the lofty chestnut, or that tree
That extends its great shade over Jupiter's grove
Of oaks the Greeks thought of as oracles,
Rise up from seeds that have fallen to the ground;
Others, such as the elm and cherry, are born
Of the undergrowth that proliferates from the root
Of the parent tree; Parnassus's laurel begins
As a little thing in the great shade of its mother.

hos natura modos primum dedit, his genus omne
silvarum fruticumque viret nemorumque sacrorum.
Sunt alii, quos ipse via sibi repperit usus.
hic plantas tenero abscindens de corpore matrum
deposuit sulcis, hic stirpes obruit arvo
quadrifidasque sudes et acuto robore vallos;
silvarumque aliae pressos propaginis arcus
exspectant et viva sua plantaria terra;
nil radicis egent aliae summumque putator
haud dubitat terrae referens mandare cacumen.
quin et caudicibus sectis (mirabile dictu)
truditur e sicco radix oleagina ligno.
et saepe alterius ramos impune videmus
vertere in alterius, mutatamque insita mala
ferre pirum et prunis lapidosa rubescere corna.
Quare agite o proprios generatim discite cultus,
agricolae, fructusque feros mollite colendo,
neu segnes iaceant terrae. iuvat Ismara Baccho
conserere atque olea magnum vestire Taburnum.
tuque ades inceptumque una decurre laborem,
o decus, o famae merito pars maxima nostrae,
Maecenas, pelagoque volans da vela patenti.

These are the ways that nature has provided
For leafy forests, sacred groves, and orchards.

Experience has found there are other ways:
One farmer breaks off shoots from the parent trunk,
Puts down the little stems into the earth,
First having taken a knife and carefully split
The buried end of the stems, or sharpened them
To help the earth more easily receive them;
There are trees with branches that wait to be arched over
And planted still alive in their own earth,
After a time developing new roots;
Some need no roots and the pruner simply cuts
A budding branch from somewhere high in the tree
And sticks it into the ground, and there it grows.
And sometimes, amazing to say it, when you cut open
The rotting stump of an old dead olive tree,
Lo and behold, a new young olive root
Has thrust its way forth! And often we have seen
How shamelessly the branches of one tree
Have turned into the branches of another,
The altered pear tree bearing grafted apples,
Or stony cornels reddening on a plum tree.
Therefore, O farmers, learn what you have to know,
The appropriate way to cultivate each kind,
To discipline their wildness, make them tame;
Don't let your land lie uselessly unused.
It is a joy to cover with vines the slopes
Of Mount Ismára and a joy to adorn
The sides of great Tabúrnus with olive trees.

Maecénas, you whose favor is my pride,
O you whose merit plays the greatest part
In all the honor I have had, Maecénas,
Come, spread sail, make haste across the sea.
I could not hope my song could tell it all,
All that there is to tell, not if I had
A hundred tongues or mouths, a voice of iron.
Come, coast along the shore, the land is near.

non ego cuncta meis amplecti versibus opto,
non mihi si linguae centum sint oraque centum,
ferrea vox. ades et primi lege litoris oram;
in manibus terrae: non hic te carmine ficto
atque per ambages et longa exorsa tenebo.

    Sponte sua quae se tollunt in luminis oras,
infecunda quidem, sed laeta et fortia surgunt;
quippe solo natura subest. tamen haec quoque, si quis
inserat aut scrobibus mandet mutata subactis,
exuerint silvestrem animum, cultuque frequenti
in quascumque voles artes haud tarda sequentur.
nec non et sterilis quae stirpibus exit ab imis,
hoc faciat, vacuos si sit digesta per agros:
nunc altae frondes et rami matris opacant
crescentique adimunt fetus uruntque ferentem.
iam quae seminibus iactis se sustulit arbos,
tarda venit, seris factura nepotibus umbram,
pomaque degenerant sucos oblita priores
et turpis avibus praedam fert uva racemos.

    Scilicet omnibus est labor impendendus et omnes
cogendae in sulcum ac multa mercede domandae.
sed truncis oleae melius, propagine vites
respondent, solido Paphiae de robore myrtus;
plantis edurae coryli nascuntur et ingens
fraxinus Herculeaeque arbos umbrosa coronae,
Chaoniique patris glandes; etiam ardua palma
nascitur et casus abies visura marinos.

Nor will our journey together be hindered by
Inordinate prefacing, fanciful songs, circuitous
Wanderings here and there among the byways.

The trees that rise up of their own free will
Into the light, wild, happy in the strength
They got from nature's power in the earth,
Do not bear fruit of their own spontaneous selves;
But if they're grafted, or taken up and replanted,
In holes that have been carefully prepared,
They'll give up their wildness, and, with frequent tilling,
Be ready to learn whatever you want them to learn.
It's just that way if you cut a barren stem
From low down on a tree and transplant it out
In an open sunlit field; left as it was,
It would be overshadowed by the abundant
Leaves and branches of its mother tree,
And its blighted berries would shrivel and dry up,
Even as they tried to grow. And the tree that arises
From seeds that fell and scattered on the ground
Develops slowly and lives to give its shade
To many later generations; its fruit
Is degenerate, having long ago forgotten
Its ancient taste, and it hangs in unsightly clusters,
Fit for nothing but for birds to ransack.

In every case hard work goes into the task
Of ordering the trees, a lot of work
To bring them under control. Stakes are the best
Supports for olives, and layering's best for vines,
Myrtles do best when the solid stem is planted;
You can propagate the hazel, whose wood is so hard,
From little slips; also the poplar tree,
Whose leaves Hercules plucked to make his crown;
So too the great Chaonian oak; the towering
Palm tree grows from slips; and the silver fir
That's born to know the dangers of the seas.

inseritur vero et nucis arbutus horrida fetu,
et steriles platani malos gessere valentis;
castaneae fagus, ornusque incanuit albo
flore piri, glandemque sues fregere sub ulmis.
   Nec modus inserere atque oculos imponere simplex.
nam qua se medio trudunt de cortice gemmae
et tenuis rumpunt tunicas, augustus in ipso
fit nodo sinus; huc aliena ex arbore germen
includunt udoque docent inolescere libro.
aut rursum enodes trunci resecantur et alte
finditur in solidum cuneis via, deinde feraces
plantae immittuntur: nec longum tempus, et ingens
exiit ad caelum ramis felicibus arbos,
miratastque novas frondes et non sua poma.
   Praeterea genus haud unum nec fortibus ulmis
nec salici lotoque neque Idaeis cyparissis,
nec pingues unam in faciem nascuntur olivae,
orchades et radii et amara pausia baca,
pomaque et Alcinoi silvae, nec surculus idem
Crustumiis Syriisque piris gravigusque volemis.
non eadem arboribus pendet vindemia nostris,
quam Methymnaeo carpit de palmite Lesbos;
sunt Thasiae vites, sunt et Mareotides albae,

But the bearded wild arbutus can be grafted
With a walnut shoot; and the sterile plane has often
Been seen to carry vigorous apple boughs;
White chestnut flowers have blossomed on the beech;
Pear-tree flowers have blossomed on the ash;
And swine have fed on acorns under the elm.

Stock-grafting and bud-grafting aren't the same:
In the place on a tree where the buds are just emerging
And breaking through their tender sheaths, a thin
Incision is cut, just at that place, and then
A bud from another tree is introduced
Into that slit, where the bark is full of sap,
And it's taught to grow and develop where it is.
In the instance of stock-grafting the cut is made
Where knots are absent, and therefore wedges are used
To open a path deep into the solid wood,
And then a slip from some fruitful other tree
Is introduced, and it isn't long before
A new great tree is towering toward the sky,
Exulting in its boughs, and full of wonder
At its foliage and its fruit, so unfamiliar.

And furthermore, all sturdy elms are not
The same as all the others, nor all willows,
All lotuses, all cypresses of Ida;
All olives aren't the same in how they're grown,
Orchad, radius, bitter Pausian;
All apples aren't alike, or the fruit that grows
In the gardens of Alcínous; Syrian pears
And Crustúmian voléma, the big pear
Shaped as if by the hollow of the hand—
None of these is grown from the same cuttings.
The grapes we gather from our vines are not
The same as those they gather from the vines
Of Lesbos; there are the vines of Thasos, and
The Mareotic vines—rich soil is right

pinguibus hae terris habiles, levioribus illae,
et passo Psithia utilior tenuisque Lageos,
temptatura pedes olim vincturaque linguam,
purpureae preciaeque, et quo te carmine dicam
Rhaetica? nec cellis ideo contende Falernis.
sunt et Aminneae vites, firmissima vina,
Tmolius adsurgit quibus et rex ipse Phanaeus;
Argitisque minor, cui non certaverit ulla
aut tantum fluere aut totidem durare per annos.
non ego te, dis et mensis accepta secundis,
transierim, Rhodia, et tumidis, Bumaste, racemis.
sed neque quam multae species nec nomina quae sint,
est numerus: neque enim numero comprendere refert;
quem qui scire velit, Libyci velit aequoris idem
discere quam multae Zephyro turbentur harenae,
aut ubi navigiis violentior incidit Eurus,
nosse quot Ionii veniant ad litora fluctus.
    Nec vero terrae ferre omnes omnia possunt.
fluminibus salices crassisque paludibus alni
nascuntur, steriles saxosis montibus orni;
litora myrtetis laetissima; denique apertos
Bacchus amat colles, Aquilonem et frigora taxi.
aspice et extremis domitum cultoribus orbem
Eoasque domos Arabum pictosque Gelonos:
divisae arboribus patriae. sola India nigrum
fert hebenum, solis est turea virga Sabaeis.
quid tibi odorato referam sudantia ligno
balsamaque et bacas semper frondentis acanthi?

For the one, less rich for the other; Psithian grapes
Are best for raisin wine; the subtle Lagéan's
Likely to tie up your feet or tangle your tongue;
The Rhaetic wine, the Purple, and the Precian—
How shall my song be adequate to them?
Yet none of these can rival the Falernian.
And then there are the Aminnáean vines,
Producers of the most full-bodied wine,
To which the Timólian defers, and even the royal
Phanean wine of Chios; and the wine
Called Lesser Argítis, outdoing all the others
In staying power and magnitude of yield.
Nor, vine of Rhodes, so pleasing at the table,
Be it of gods or men, for the second course,
Would I omit my praise of you, nor you,
Full-breasted clusters of Bumástus. And yet
There are so many kinds, so many names,
I couldn't possibly hope to list them all.
To try to do so would be tantamount
To trying to count how many grains of sand
Whirl up when the West Wind strikes the Libyan desert,
Or, when the raging East Wind falls upon
The ships at sea, how many waves come in
To break and shatter on the Ionian shore.

However, to tell the truth, not everything
Can grow in every place. Thus, willows grow
By rivers, alders in boggy swamps, the sterile
Ash tree grows on rocky mountainsides;
The seashore loves to have the myrtle grow there,
And Bacchus loves the gentle open hills;
The yew tree loves the cold North Wind; and think
Of those regions out at the farthest boundaries,
Conquered by planting and tilling, the Eastern countries
Of Arabs and tattooed Gelónians;
Different trees have different regions to grow in.
Black ebony grows in India alone,
Frankincense only where the Sabaeans dwell.
Why tell of the balsam oozing from the bark

quid nemora Aethiopum molli canentia lana,
velleraque ut foliis depectant tenuia Seres?
aut quos Oceano propior gerit India lucos,
extremi sinus orbis, ubi aëra vincere summum
arboris haud ullae iactu potuere sagittae?
et gens illa quidem sumptis non tarda pharetris.
Media fert tristis sucos tardumque saporem
felicis mali, quo non praesentius ullum,
pocula si quando saevae infecere novercae
miscueruntque herbas et non innoxia verba,
auxilium venit ac membris agit atra venena.
ipsa ingens arbos faciemque simillima lauro
(et, si non alium late iactaret odorem,
laurus erat); folia haud ullis labentia ventis;
flos ad prima tenax; animas et olentia Medi
ora fovent illo et senibus medicantur anhelis.

    Sed neque Medorum silvae, ditissima terra,
nec pulcher Ganges atque auro turbidus Hermus
laudibus Italiae certent, non Bactra neque Indi
totaque turiferis Panchaia pinguis harenis.
haec loca non tauri spirantes naribus ignem
invertere satis immanis dentibus hydri,
nec galeis densisque virum seges horruit hastis;
sed gravidae fruges et Bacchi Massicus umor
implevere; tenent oleae armentaque laeta.

Of its aromatic wood? Why tell of the berries
Of the always leafy acanthus, or the groves
Of Ethiopia, white with the wool that grows
On the wool-bearing tree, or those of the Seres, who comb
Their fine silk down from the branches of the silk tree?
Why tell of that farthermost region of India,
Out at the end of the world, out next to the ocean,
Where the trees are so tall that no one can shoot an arrow
Beyond those high treetops, although the natives
Are skillful with the bow? In Media there grows
The citron tree with its restorative fruit,
Sour in taste and aftertaste. Suppose
Your cruel stepmother, one day, poisons your cup,
Muttering spells as she mixes in the herbs,
The juice of this fruit will come to your body's aid,
Expelling the deadly venom from your veins.
The tree is big and closely resembles the laurel;
Indeed, if it weren't for the different fragrance it sheds
It might well *be* a laurel tree; no winds
Bring down its leaves and its blossom is tenacious;
The Mede makes use of it to sweeten his breath
And as medicine for an old man's wheezing breathing.

Not Media with its fabulous rich forests,
Nor the beautiful river Ganges, nor the Hermus,
The very mud of whose riverbed is gold,
Can bear comparison with Italy;
Not Bactria, nor India, nor all
Arabia with its perfumed sands. No teams
Of bulls with nostrils breathing fire have dragged
Their plows across our fields to get them ready
For sowing the monster teeth of the Hydra dragon,
Nor in our fields has there ever bristled up
A yield of ranks of helmeted men and lances.
Our fields are filled with crops abundantly growing,
Our vineyards with the grapes of Bacchus's Massic;
Our country is the home of olive groves,

hinc bellator equus campo sese arduus infert,
hinc albi, Clitumne, greges et maxima taurus
victima, saepe tuo perfusi flumine sacro,
Romanos ad templa deum duxere triumphos.
hic ver adsiduum atque alienis mensibus aestas:
bis gravidae pecudes, bis pomis utilis arbos.
at rabidae tigres absunt et saeva leonum
semina, nec miseros fallunt aconita legentis,
nec rapit immensos orbis per humum neque tanto
squameus in spiram tractu se colligit anguis.
adde tot egregias urbes operumque laborem,
tot congesta manu praeruptis oppida saxis
fluminaque antiquos subterlabentia muros.
an mare, quod supra, memorem, quodque adluit infra?
anne lacus tantos? te, Lari maxime, teque,
fluctibus et fremitu adsurgens Benace marino?
an memorem portus Lucrinoque addita claustra
atque indignatum magnis stridoribus aequor,
Iulia qua ponto longe sonat unda refuso
Tyrrhenusque fretis immittitur aestus Avernis?
haec eadem argenti rivos aerisque metalla
ostendit venis atque auro plurima fluxit.
haec genus acre virum, Marsos pubemque Sabellam
adsuetumque malo Ligurem Volscosque verutos
extulit, haec Decios, Marios magnosque Camillos,

The place where flocks and herds prospering dwell.
Hence on our plains the proud war horse steps forth;
Hence, River Clitúmnus, bathed in your sacred stream,
The herds emerge snow-white to graze in the fields,
And the great majestic bull is sacrificed
At the triumphs at the temple of the gods.
Here spring outlasts itself and summer goes on
Beyond the months allotted to itself;
Twice every year our livestock bear their young,
And twice a year our trees yield us their fruit.
We have no ravening tigers here, nor any
Lions here to spawn ferocious offspring;
No deadly poison aconite to trick
The unfortunate unwary one who picks it;
No snake that winds his giant length along,
Or gathers his scaly self around himself
In a coil within a coil within a coil.

And then there are so many wonderful cities,
That so much toil has built, and all those towns
The hand of man has made, high up upon
The rocky cliffs above the mountain streams
That flow along beneath their ancient walls.
Nor should I fail to sing of the mighty lakes,
Of you, great Lárius, or, Benácus, you
Whose waters roar and seethe like ocean waters?
Nor shall my song forget to tell of her harbors
And the clamorous protests of the ocean waves
As the great seawall was built at Lake Lucrínus,
And the echoing sounds were heard from far when the waters,
Repulsed and baffled, were turned and driven into
The channel cut to take them to Lake Avérnus.
Nor shall I forget our veins of silver and copper,
And the gold that flows in our rivers, lavishly.

This land has engendered a powerful progeny:
The Marsians, the Sabines, the Ligúrians,
Experienced in putting up with hardship,
The Volscian spearmen, the Marii, and the Dacians,

Scipiadas duros bello et te, maxime Caesar,
qui nunc extremis Asiae iam victor in oris
imbellem avertis Romanis arcibus Indum.
salve, magna parens frugum, Saturnia tellus,
magna virum: tibi res antiquae laudis et artem
ingredior, sanctos ausus recludere fontis,
Ascraeumque cano Romana per oppida carmen.
    Nunc locus arvorum ingeniis, quae robora cuique,
quis color et quae sit rebus natura ferendis.
difficiles primum terrae collesque maligni,
tenuis ubi argilla et dumosis calculus arvis,
Palladia gaudent silva vivacis olivae.
indicio est tractu surgens oleaster eodem
plurimus et strati bacis silvestribus agri.
at quae pinguis humus dulcique uligine laeta,
quique frequens herbis et fertilis ubere campus
(qualem saepe cava montis convalle solemus
despicere; huc summis liquuntur rupibus amnes
felicemque trahunt limum) quique editus Austro
et filicem curvis invisam pascit aratris:
hic tibi praevalidas olim multoque fluentis
sufficiet Baccho vitis, hic fertilis uvae,

The stalwart-in-battle Scipios, and the great
Camilli, and you, the greatest of all, O Caesar,
Victor in Asia out to its farthest limits—
And now you have driven the cowardly Indian off
And far away from the seven hills of Rome.

Then hail, Saturnian land, great mother of men,
Great mother of teeming crops. I undertake
In honor of you a task that from ancient days
Has won such praise because it required such skill,
Daring to break the seal on the sacred spring
And sing Hesiod's song in Roman towns.

&

We turn now to the subject of the nature
Of different kinds of soil, their strengths, their color,
What each of them is best at bringing forth.
First of all, where the ground's intractable
And the hills unwelcoming, with thorns in the fields,
The earth a thin white clay, with a lot of gravel,
Such a terrain is pleased with Minerva's grove
Of hardy tenacious long-lived olive trees.
It's typical of such places that you'll find
A plethora of oleasters thriving,
And their wild berries scattered everywhere.

But a place that's level, and with fertile soil,
Luxurious in having an abundance
Of sweet-tasting water, and with plenty of green
Herbage and the nutriments it yields
(For instance, on the floor of a mountain valley
That mountain torrents come down to from the heights,
Bringing rich sediment with them as they come),
And that faces south, and sponsors the growth of ferns,
Those enemies of the curved blade of the plow,
Such places promise the hardiest and the most
Prosperous of vines, from which will flow
The beneficial streams of Bacchus's gifts,

hic laticis, qualem pateris libamus et auro,
inflavit cum pinguis ebur Tyrrhenus ad aras,
lancibus et pandis fumantia reddimus exta.

Sin armenta magis studium vitulosque tueri,
aut ovium fetum aut urentis culta capellas,
saltus et saturi petito longinqua Tarenti,
et qualem infelix amisit Mantua campum,
pascentem niveos herboso flumine cycnos:
non liquidi gregibus fontes, non gramina derunt,
et quantum longis carpent armenta diebus,
exigua tantum gelidus ros nocte reponet.

Nigra fere et presso pinguis sub vomere terra
et cui putre solum (namque hoc imitamur arando),
optima frumentis: non ullo ex aequore cernes
plura domum tardis decedere plaustra iuvencis:
aut unde iratus silvam devexit arator
et nemora evertit multos ignava per annos,
antiquasque domos avium cum stirpibus imis
eruit; illae altum nidis petiere relictis,
at rudis enituit impulso vomere campus.
nam ieiuna quidem clivosi glarea ruris
vix humilis apibus casias roremque ministrat,
et tofus scaber et nigris exesa chelydris
creta negant alios aeque serpentibus agros

Life-giving in the grape, and in the wine
In the golden bowl we pour a libation from,
As the elegant Etruscan at the altar
Blows his horn, and as from massive platters
The steaming sacrifice is offered up.

If taking care of cattle and their calves
Is what you do, or raising sheep, or goats
(That devastate the crops), then you should seek
Wealthy Tárentum's glades and hilly meadows,
Or plains like those unfortunate Mantua lost,
Where snow-white swans feed on the grassy river.
In such a place there will be ample pastures
And clear refreshing springs for your flocks to drink from;
And what your herds have cropped all one long day
The cool dew will restore in one short night.

A rich black soil that's crumbling even before
The pressure of the plowshare's felt upon it
(So that the plowing almost seems to mimic
A plowing that has already taken place)—
A soil like that is almost always the best
For growing grain. Nowhere else will you see
So many loaded wagons making their way
Slowly back to their homes behind their bullocks.
Or there's the land the angry plowman clears
By cutting down the groves that stood untouched
For many years, and carrying off the wood,
And pulling up the roots of the ancient homes
Of birds that now unnested seek the sky,
And the virgin field lies shining under the plowshare.

But in hilly places where the soil is meager,
Nothing but gravel, a few scanty bushes
Of rosemary and marjoram are barely
Enough for the bees; and the rough porous tufa
And the chalk that the venomous water snakes eat out

dulcem ferre cibum et curvas praebere latebras.
quae tenuem exhalat nebulam fumosque volucres
et bibit umorem et, cum vult, ex se ipsa remittit,
quaeque suo semper viridi se gramine vestit,
nec scabie et salsa laedit robigine ferrum,
illa tibi laetis intexet vitibus ulmos,
illa ferax oleae est, illam experiere colendo
et facilem pecori et patientem vomeris unci.
talem dives arat Capua et vicina Vesaevo
ora iugo et vacuis Clanius non aequus Acerris.
    Nunc quo quamque modo possis cognoscere dicam.
rara sit an supra morem si densa requires
(altera frumentis quoniam favet, altera Baccho,
densa magis Cereri, rarissima quaeque Lyaeo),
ante locum capies oculis, alteque iubebis
in solido puteum demitti, omnemque repones
rursus humum et pedibus summas aequabis harenas.
si derunt, rarum pecorique et vitibus almis
aptius uber erit; sin in sua posse negabunt
ire loca et scrobibus superabit terra repletis,
spissus ager: glaebas cunctantis crassaque terga
exspecta et validis terram proscinde iuvencis.
salsa autem tellus et quae perhibetur amara

Deny that any other place provides
Snake food as sweet as this or better holes
For snakes to wind into, to hide themselves.
But if the soil breathes steaming vapors out,
Drinks moisture in, and when it wants to, breathes
The moisture out again, and if it's always
Green with the greenness of its grasses, and
Never corrodes the blade of the plow with rust,
Then that's the place to drape your flourishing vines
Upon your elms, the place that will produce
Rich olive oil, the place (as the tilling will show)
That makes the plowing easy for the beasts
Because the soil is easy for the plow.
And this is what the land is like for plowing
At Capua and near Vesuvius
And along the sides of the river Clanius,
Hostile to deserted Ácerráe.

Now I'll describe the methods to use to tell
The different kinds of soil from one another.
If you want to determine if your soil is lighter
Than usual, or on the other hand denser—
The denser better for Ceres, the lighter for Bacchus—
Find a convenient spot and have your workers
Dig out a big pit in the solid ground,
Then have them shovel the dirt they dug back in
And trample it down with their feet until it's level.
If it doesn't entirely fill the hole, it's light,
And best for pasture or the kindly vine;
But if they can't get all the dirt back in,
And some of it's left over, then it's dense,
And you can expect there will be stubborn glebes,
Thick, clodded—heavy going—calling for
The oxen's weight and strength to break them up.

Then there's the salty soil known as the "bitter,"
Unhappy for crops, untamable by the plow;

(frugibus infelix ea, nec mansuescit arando
nec Baccho genus aut pomis sua nomina servat),
tale dabit specimen: tu spisso vimine qualos
colaque prelorum fumosis deripe tectis;
huc ager ille malus dulcesque a fontibus undae
ad plenum calcentur; aqua eluctabitur omnis
scilicet et grandes ibunt per vimina guttae;
at sapor indicium faciet manifestus, et ora
tristia temptantum sensu torquebit amaro.
pinguis item quae sit tellus, hoc denique pacto
discimus: haud umquam manibus iactata fatiscit,
sed picis in morem ad digitos lentescit habendo.
umida maiores herbas alit, ipsaque iusto
laetior. a, nimium ne sit mihi fertilis illa,
nec se praevalidam primis ostendat aristis!
quae gravis est, ipso tacitam se pondere prodit,
quaeque levis. promptum est oculis praediscere nigram,
et quis cui color. at sceleratum exquirere frigus
difficile est: piceae tantum taxique nocentes
interdum aut hederae pandunt vestigia nigrae.

His animadversis terram multo ante memento
excoquere et magnos scrobibus concidere montis,
ante supinatas Aquiloni ostendere glaebas,
quam laetum infodias vitis genus. optima putri
arva solo: id venti curant gelidaeque pruinae

The best of vines produce new generations
Unworthy of their lines; the reputations
Of the most illustrious families of fruits
Are ill served here. To test for it, do this:
Take a closely woven wicker basket down
From the smoky roof of your house, and fill it up
With this questionable soil, and then pour in
Fresh water from the spring; you'll see the water
Make its way through, and the big drops fall into
The receptacle below; then taste the water;
The taste will tell the story: the taster's mouth
Grimacing from the bitter taste of it.

And this is the only way to tell if a soil
Is rich or not: when you work it with your hands
Rich soil won't fall apart; instead, it's sticky
And pliable in your hands the way pitch is.
Moist soil fosters over-luxuriant foliage,
Being more fertile than it ought to be.
(Ah, not for me that too-prolific earth!
Let it not be too strong when the ears are new!)
A heavy soil will silently demonstrate
How heavy it is by how heavy it feels in your hands;
A light soil too, by its lightness in your hands.
The eye can easily see which soil is black
And which some other color, but it's hard
To tell by looking whether or not the soil
Is of the cursed cold sort; only the presence
Of pine, black ivy, or the sinister yew,
Perhaps, sometimes, will tell you that it's there.

❧

Having considered all these things, take care
To cut through the ridges of turf and lay the ground
Open to wind and sun to bake it dry,
All this before you plant the joyous vine.
The luckiest fields are those with crumbly soil—
The winds and frosts will have taken care of it,

et labefacta movens robustus iugera fossor.
at si quos haud ulla viros vigilantia fugit,
ante locum similem exquirunt, ubi prima paretur
arboribus seges et quo mox digesta feratur,
mutatam ignorent subito ne semina matrem.
quin etiam caeli regionem in cortice signant,
ut quo quaeque modo steterit, qua parte calores
austrinos tulerit, quae terga obverterit axi,
restituant: adeo in teneris consuescere multum est.
    Collibus an plano melius sit ponere vitem,
quaere prius. si pinguis agros metabere campi,
densa sere; in denso non segnior ubere Bacchus:
sin tumulis adclive solum collesque supinos,
indulge ordinibus; nec setius omnis in unguem
arboribus positis secto via limite quadret.
ut saepe ingenti bello cum longa cohortis
explicuit legio et campo stetit agmen aperto,
derectaeque acies, ac late fluctuat omnis
aere renidenti tellus, necdum horrida miscent
proelia, sed dubius mediis Mars errat in armis:
omnia sint paribus numeris dimensa viarum;
non animum modo uti pascat prospectus inanem,
sed quia non aliter vires dabit omnibus aequas

And the sturdy laborer, too, whose task it is
To loosen up the ground in preparation.
But men who are so careful that nothing escapes
Their vigilant attention also look
For fields that closely resemble one another
(One, the nursery for the little vines
That the trees around them support, the other to which
The vines at the proper time can be carried over
And planted out), so that the vines won't think,
Because of this sudden change from place to place,
That they've been taken from their mother. Indeed,
These men notate in the bark of the trees exactly
Which region of the sky each plant faced toward,
So in the new field, replanted, they occupy
The same position as in the nursery,
Facing the warmth of the south in just the same way,
Their backs to the northern cold just as before—
Such is the need, when young, of what's familiar.

But first you have to decide whether it's better
To plant your vines on hills or the level plain.
If the ground is level, plant them close together;
Bacchus is not less generous where they're planted
Closely in that fashion. But if the ground's hilly,
Terraced or sloping upward, set them out widely.
Whatever the terrain, be sure to place them
So that the paths between them are always the same;
Space out the plantings with exactitude,
As when before the battle the cohorts are all
Deployed and ready, rank after regular rank,
The gleam of steel reflecting the gleam of steel
Across the plain as far as the eye can see,
And Mars, the god of war, not yet decided
Which army will be the victor, walks between them.
Just so, deploy your vines in equal numbers
So that the lines are uniform and straight,
Not merely for the pleasure of the prospect
But so the soil may give its strength to all

terra neque in vacuum poterunt se extendere rami.
    Forsitan et scrobibus quae sint fastigia quaeras.
ausim vel tenui vitem committere sulco.
altior ac penitus terrae defigitur arbos,
aesculus in primis, quae quantum vertice ad auras
aetherias, tantum radice in Tartara tendit.
ergo non hiemes illam, non flabra neque imbres
convellunt; immota manet, multosque nepotes,
multa virum volvens durando saecula vincit.
tum fortis late ramos et bracchia tendens
huc illuc, media ipsa ingentem sustinet umbram.
    Neve tibi ad solem vergant vineta cadentem,
neve inter vitis corylum sere, neve flagella
summa pete aut summa defringe ex arbore plantas
(tantus amor terrae), neu ferro laede retunso
semina, neve oleae silvestris insere truncos.
nam saepe incautis pastoribus excidit ignis,
qui furtim pingui primum sub cortice tectus
robora comprendit, frondesque elapsus in altas
ingentem caelo sonitum dedit; inde secutus
per ramos victor perque alta cacumina regnat,
et totum involvit flammis nemus et ruit atram
ad caelum picea crassus caligine nubem,
praesertim si tempestas a vertice silvis
incubuit, glomeratque ferens incendia ventus.
hoc ubi, non a stirpe valent caesaeque reverti
possunt atque ima similes revirescere terra;
infelix superat foliis oleaster amaris.

The vines in equal measure and their branches
Freely extend themselves upon the air.

Perhaps the question is, how deep to dig
The holes for planting: I'd trust a shallow trench
For vines; for trees, much deeper into the earth—
Especially the great oak tree, whose roots
Reach down as far into the Underworld
As its crown extends into the ethereal sky.
Therefore no winter tempest, wind or rain,
Can bring it down; it stands where it is, unmoved,
And generations pass, and still it's there,
Holding its great arms out, and towering there
Enveloped in the darkness of its leaves.

Don't plant your vineyard sloping toward the sunset;
Don't plant the hazel, with its spreading roots,
Among the vines; never break off the topmost
Tendrils of the vines (that love the earth);
Don't bruise your tender plants with a blunt knife.
And never graft your olives to oleasters.
It has been known to happen that a neglectful
Shepherd has failed to see that a spark has lingered
From a fire he thought he'd finished with, and so
It catches under the bark of an olive tree,
And burns at first unnoticed there, and then
Takes hold of the trunk, flows up to the leaves above,
And sending a huge roar up into the sky,
Then rages conquering, victorious,
Through all the treetop branches of the grove,
With thick black viscous smoke-clouds churning upwards.
Such an event is worst of all if a storm
Comes crashing down from the heavens, its wind creating
A fire ball of the flames already burning.
When something like this happens there isn't strength
Enough in the roots of the smitten olive trees
To help them rise from the earth to flourish again;
The barren oleaster alone survives.

Nec tibi tam prudens quisquam persuadeat auctor
tellurem Borea rigidam spirante movere.
rura gelu tunc claudit hiems nec semine iacto
concretam patitur radicem adfigere terrae.
optima vinetis satio, cum vere rubente
candida venit avis longis invisa colubris,
prima vel autumni sub frigora, cum rapidus Sol
nondum hiemem contingit equis, iam praeterit aestas.
ver adeo frondi nemorum, ver utile silvis,
vere tument terrae et genitalia semina poscunt.
tum pater omnipotens fecundis imbribus Aether
coniugis in gremium laetae descendit, et omnis
magnus alit magno commixtus corpore fetus.
avia tum resonant avibus virgulta canoris,
et Venerem certis repetunt armenta diebus;
parturit almus ager Zephyrique tepentibus auris
laxant arva sinus; superat tener omnibus umor,
inque novos soles audent se gramina tuto
credere, nec metuit surgentis pampinus Austros
aut actum caelo magnis Aquilonibus imbrem,
sed trudit gemmas et frondes explicat omnis.
non alios prima crescentis origine mundi
inluxisse dies aliumve habuisse tenorem
crediderim: ver illud erat, ver magnus agebat
orbis et hibernis parcebant flatibus Euri,
cum primae lucem pecudes hausere, virumque
terrea progenies duris caput extulit arvis,

Don't let yourself be advised to plow the rigid
Soil of your field when the cold North Wind is blowing;
It's winter then and the land is seized in frost;
The ground refuses to accept the frozen
Root of the young plant if you plant it then.
The very best time to set your young vines out
Is at the moment when spring begins to blush
And the white stork, who's the scourge of snakes, is seen;
Or the moment when summer has just begun to pass,
And just before the first cold day of autumn,
When the chariot of summer and its warmth
Has not yet reached the edge of the coming winter.

It's spring that adorns the woods and groves with leaves;
In spring the soil, desiring seed, is tumid,
And then the omnipotent father god descends
In showers from the sky and enters into
The joyful bridal body of the earth,
His greatness and her greatness in their union
Bringing to life the life waiting to live.
Birdsong is heard in every secluded thicket,
And all the beasts of the field have become aware
That love's appointed days have come again.
The generous earth is ready to give birth
And the meadows ungirdle for Zephyr's warming breezes;
The tender dew is there on everything;
The new grass dares entrust itself to the new
Suns of the new days and the little tendrils
Of the young vines have no fear of a South Wind coming
Nor of a North Wind from a stormy sky;
The vine brings forth its buds; its leaves unfold.
I think it must have been that just such days
As these were the shining days when the world was new;
Everywhere it was spring, the whole world over;
The East Wind held in check its winter winds;
The beasts drank in the light of that first dawn;
The first men, born of the earth, raised up their heads
From the stony ground; the woods were stocked with game,
And the first stars came out in the sky above.

immissaeque ferae silvis et sidera caelo.
nec res hunc tenerae possent perferre laborem,
si non tanta quies iret frigusque caloremque
inter, et exciperet caeli indulgentia terras.

Quod superest, quaecumque premes virgulta per agros,
sparge fimo pingui et multa memor occule terra,
aut lapidem bibulum aut squalentis infode conchas;
inter enim labentur aquae, tenuisque subibit
halitus atque animos tollent sata. iamque reperti,
qui saxo super atque ingentis pondere testae
urgerent: hoc effusos munimen ad imbres,
hoc, ubi hiulca siti findit Canis aestifer arva.

Seminibus positis superest diducere terram
saepius ad capita et duros iactare bidentis,
aut presso exercere solum sub vomere et ipsa
flectere luctantis inter vineta iuvencos;
tum levis calamos et rasae hastilia virgae
fraxineasque aptare sudes furcasque valentis,
viribus eniti quarum et contemnere ventos
adsuescant summasque sequi tabulata per ulmos.

Ac dum prima novis adolescit frondibus aetas,
parcendum teneris, et dum se laetus ad auras
palmes agit laxis per purum immissus habenis,
ipsa acie nondum falcis temptanda, sed uncis
carpendae manibus frondes interque legendae.
inde ubi iam validis amplexae stirpibus ulmos
exierint, tum stringe comas, tum bracchia tonde
(ante reformidant ferrum), tum denique dura
exerce imperia et ramos compesce fluentis.

Nor could the tender plants endure their lot
If spring's relief were not to intervene
Between the heat of summer and winter's cold.

And, in addition, manure your plantings with dung,
And be sure to cover them well, with plenty of soil;
And maybe put porous stones or broken shells
In the hole with them, so moisture will find its way,
And air will find its way, to the little vines,
To give them encouragement. It's not unheard of
To lay down heavy stones or heavy jars
Over the plantings, protection from drenching rain
Or on the days when fields lie cracked and gaping
Under the heat of Canícula the Dog Star.
The young vines having been set in place, be sure
To keep the earth well loosened around the roots,
Either by using your heavy hoe to work it,
Or else with your plow, turning your laboring beasts
This way, then that way, between the rows of vines;
Then fashion shafts and stakes and forks from ash
And cane and reeds and such, to make a trellis
Or ladder to which the vines will learn to cling
And climb from tier to tier up to the top
Of their supporting elms, scorning the winds.

While they're still very young, their leaves just new,
Go easy with them, respect their tenderness,
And while the tendril, joyful, puts itself forth,
Reaching up skyward into the air, unfettered,
Do not attack the vine as yet with your knife,
But carefully, with your fingers, pluck and pick;
And then when the vine has grown, embracing the elms
With stronger stems, the time has come when you
—Before they're wary of the pruning knife—
Can strip away locks and clip off clinging arms,
Enforcing your stern dominion to restrain
The overflowing profusion of the branches.

Texendae saepes etiam et pecus omne tenendum,
praecipue dum frons tenera imprudensque laborum;
cui super indignas hiemes solemque potentem
silvestres uri adsidue capreaeque sequaces
inludunt, pascuntur oves avidaeque iuvencae.
frigora nec tantum cana concreta pruina
aut gravis incumbens scopulis arentibus aestas,
quantum illi nocuere greges durique venenum
dentis et admorso signata in stirpe cicatrix.
non aliam ob culpam Baccho caper omnibus aris
caeditur et veteres ineunt proscaenia ludi,
praemiaque ingeniis pagos et compita circum
Thesidae posuere, atque inter pocula laeti
mollibus in pratis unctos saluere per utres.
nec non Ausonii, Troia gens missa, coloni
versibus incomptis ludunt risuque soluto,
oraque corticibus sumunt horrenda cavatis,
et te, Bacche, vocant per carmina laeta, tibique
oscilla ex alta suspendunt mollia pinu.
hinc omnis largo pubescit vinea fetu,
complentur vallesque cavae saltusque profundi
et quocumque deus circum caput egit honestum.
ergo rite suum Baccho dicemus honorem
carminibus patriis lancesque et liba feremus,
et ductus cornu stabit sacer hircus ad aram,
pinguiaque in veribus torrebimus exta colurnis.
    Est etiam ille labor curandis vitibus alter,
cui numquam exhausti satis est: namque omne quotannis
terque quaterque solum scindendum glaebaque versis

Then too you must be sure that there are hedges
To keep the beasts away, especially
When the leaves are young and tender, still ignorant
Of trouble and untested. Worse than winter's
Harshness and the tyranny of the sun
Are the buffalo and deer when they can get
In at the vines and make themselves free with them;
And sheep and hungry heifers feed on them too.
The coldest frost, and the most oppressive heat
That weighs down on a thirsting landscape, don't
Do half as much harm as beasts with their venomous teeth
And the scars of their gnawing on the helpless stems.

This is the crime, no other, for which the goat
Is sacrificed to Bacchus at all the altars,
And old-time stage plays had their first beginning
On such occasions, in rural villages
Or down at the nearby crossroads, with singing contests
And dancing on oiled goatskins in the meadows.
And indeed, even today, in country places,
With lots of laughing, the peasants put on fearsome
Masks made out of hollowed cork, and chant
Their uncouth verses, and, Bacchus, sing their joyful
Songs to you, and on the pine-tree branches
Hang little amulet faces that sway in the breeze.
And so the vines grow ripe and lavishly
Bring forth their fruit, and every vale and glade
Is full to overflowing, everywhere
To which the pleased god turns his beautiful face.
So, as is right for us to do, we'll sing
Our rustic songs in honor of the god,
And, taking the goat by the horn, we'll lead him up
To the sacrificial altar, and afterwards roast
The rich goat meat on spits of hazelwood.

And then there's this other work that has to be done,
The need for it never exhausted: three times a year,
Four times, you must turn the soil, to open it up,
Dragging the drag-hoe backwards, over and over,

aeternum frangenda bidentibus, omne levandum
fronde nemus. redit agricolis labor actus in orbem,
atque in se sua per vestigia volvitur annus.
ac iam olim seras posuit cum vinea frondes,
frigidus et silvis Aquilo decussit honorem,
iam tum acer curas venientem extendit in annum
rusticus, et curvo Saturni dente relictam
persequitur vitem attondens fingitque putando.
primus humum fodito, primus devecta cremato
sarmenta et vallos primus sub tecta referto;
postremus metito. bis vitibus ingruit umbra,
bis segetem densis obducunt sentibus herbae;
durus uterque labor: laudato ingentia rura,
exiguum colito. nec non etiam aspera rusti
vimina per silvam et ripis fluvialis harundo
caeditur, incultique exercet cura salicti.
iam vinctae vites, iam falcem arbusta reponunt,
iam canit effectos extremus vinitor antes:
sollicitanda tamen tellus pulvisque movendus,
et iam maturis metuendus Iuppiter uvis.
　　Contra, non ulla est oleis cultura, neque illae
procurvam exspectant falcem rastrosque tenacis,

To break up the clods; and the overgrowth of leaves
Needs to be cut away, to let the light through.
The farmer's labor circles back on him
As the seasons of the year roll back around
To where they were and walk in their own footsteps.
And just as soon as the year's old leaves have fallen
And the cold North Wind has shaken loose the lovely
Foliage of the autumn trees, the vigilant
Farmer will set himself to work preparing
For the year to come, cutting and pruning and shaping
With his curved Saturnian blade. So be the first
To dig in the ground, the first to carry away
The prunings and burn them, the first to see to it
That the poles that supported the vines are safely stowed
Out of the winter weather; be the last of all
To leave off harvesting. Two times a year
The menacing shade grows thicker on the vines;
Two times a year the thorny weeds advance;
Hard labor to fight them off in either case.
("Admire a big estate but farm a small one.")

And beyond these tasks there's still more work to be done:
Wands of sharp-pointed broom that grows in the woods
Need to be cut, and reeds from the riverbank,
The beds of wild-willow shoots need to be cared for.
And now the vines are tied, and the pruning knife
Is put aside, and now the worker sings
As he comes to the end of the last rank of the vines;
Yet after that you'll still have the work of keeping
The earth loosened up around the tied-up vines;
And still you'll have the worry of whether or not
Jupiter's storm will descend on your ripened grapes.

❧

But olive trees need nothing like such care,
Since once they've taken hold they neither expect
The harrying attentions of the mattock
Or the crooked pruning knife. Earth of herself

cum semel haeserunt arvis aurasque tulerunt;
ipsa satis tellus, cum dente recluditur unco,
sufficit umorem et gravidas, cum vomere, fruges.
hoc pinguem et placitam Paci nutritor olivam.

  Poma quoque, ut primum truncos sensere valentis
et vires habuere suas, ad sidera raptim
vi propria nituntur opisque haud indiga nostrae.
nec minus interea fetu nemus omne gravescit,
sanguineisque inculta rubent aviaria bacis.
tondentur cytisi, taedas silva alta ministrat,
pascunturque ignes nocturni et lumina fundunt.
et dubitant homines serere atque impendere curam?
quid maiora sequar? salices humilesque genistae,
aut illae pecori frondem aut pastoribus umbram
sufficiunt saepemque satis et pabula melli.
et iuvat undantem buxo spectare Cytorum
Naryciaeque picis lucos, iuvat arva videre
non rastris, hominum non ulli obnoxia curae.
ipsae Caucasio steriles in vertice silvae,
quas animosi Euri adsidue franguntque feruntque,
dant alios aliae fetus, dant utile lignum
navigiis pinos, domibus cedrumque cupressosque;
hinc radios trivere rotis, hinc tympana plaustris
agricolae, et pandas ratibus posuere carinas.
viminibus salices fecundae, frondibus ulmi,
at myrtus validis hastilibus et bona bello
cornus, Ituraeos taxi torquentur in arcus.
nec tiliae leves aut torno rasile buxum

Provides sufficient moisture and an abundant
Yield of olives, when lightly hoed or plowed.
This is the way to nurture the olive tree,
The favorite smiled upon by the goddess Peace.

And it's the same with fruit trees: once they feel
They've come into their strength and self-reliance,
They rapidly strive up toward the starry sky—
And they do so by themselves, without our labor;
And every grove meanwhile grows heavy, burdened
With burgeoning fruit, and crimson berries redden
The wild uncultivated haunts of birds;
The cytisus plant is there for cattle to browse on;
High woods yield resinous pine-tree branches for torches,
To light the nocturnal fires in people's houses—
Their hearth fires shine in the darkness of the night.

What need have I for a loftier song to sing?
The humble broom and osier can provide
Fodder for cattle and shade for the resting herdsman,
A hedge for the plants, and food for the honeybee;
It's a cause for joy, to see the box trees waving
Upon the sides of Mount Cytórus, and see
Nárycum's pitch-pine forests, and to look
At fields that never felt what the harrow does,
Nor ever were subject to human discipline.
The barren woods, high up Caucasian peaks,
Battered and torn by the angry East Wind's fury,
Nevertheless have useful things to give:
Pinewood for boats, cedar and cypress for houses,
Wood for farmers to use to make their wheel spokes,
Or to make spokeless drum-wheels, for their wagons,
And wood to make the keels for boats at sea.
The gifts the willow gives are its willow wands,
And elm its leaves; the gifts of myrtle and cornel
Are the shafts for making spears that they provide,
Weapons of war; of yew trees it's the way
Parthian bows can be made from their bent branches;
And lindens too, and boxwood, cut and shaped

non formam accipiunt ferroque cavantur acuto.
nec non et torrentem undam levis innatat alnus
missa Pado, nec non et apes examina condunt
corticibusque cavis vitiosaeque ilicis alvo.
quid memorandum aeque Baccheia dona tulerunt?
Bacchus et ad culpam causas dedit; ille furentis
Centauros leto domuit, Rhoetumque Pholumque
et magno Hylaeum Lapithis cratere minantem.

    O fortunatos nimium, sua si bona norint,
agricolas! quibus ipsa, procul discordibus armis,
fundit humo facilem victum iustissima tellus.
si non ingentem foribus domus alta superbis
mane salutantum totis vomit aedibus undam,
nec varios inhiant pulchra testudine postis
inlusasque auro vestes Ephyreiaque aera,
alba neque Assyrio fucatur lana veneno,
nec casia liquidi corrumpitur usus olivi:
at secura quies et nescia fallere vita,
dives opum variarum, at latis otia fundis,
speluncae vivique lacus et frigida Tempe
mugitusque boum mollesque sub arbore somni
non absunt; illic saltus ac lustra ferarum,
et patiens operum exiguoque adsueta iuventus,

And polished by the lathe, for various uses;
Boats are made from buoyant alderwood
To swim upon the raging waters of Po;
And swarms of bees can make their hives in hollow
Cork trees or the bellies of rotting alders.
What gifts like these has Bacchus ever brought us?
Bacchus, indeed, has given cause for blame:
He brought about the maddened Centaurs' death—
Rhóetus, Pholus, and riotous Hyláeus,
With his great wine flagon menacing the Lapiths.

O greatly fortunate farmers, if only they knew
How lucky they are! Far from the battlefield,
Earth brings forth from herself in ample justice
The simple means of life, simply enjoyed.
What if there's no great mansion from whose proud
High doors at dawn the crowd of those who came
The evening before to flatter the lord of the place
Pours out; what if the farmer has never gazed
In open-mouthed astonishment at such
Doors as those doors, adorned with tortoiseshell,
Or draperies tricked out with gold, or bronzes
Brought from Ephyraeus; what if no dye
Imported from Assyria has ever
Stained his pure white woolen cloth; what if
The clear plain daily olive oil he uses
Has never been sophisticated by
The mingling in of oil of cassia bark?
His sleep at night is easy, his life knows nothing
About deceit or trickery, and his life
Is rich in many things: tranquillity
Of the broad fields, of grottoes, and of lakes,
Of cattle lowing while in the shade of a tree
The herdsman peacefully dozes—they have all this—
They have forest glades, and haunts of beasts to hunt,
A youth accustomed to simplicity
And disciplined by work, respect for the elders,

sacra deum sanctique patres: extrema per illos
Iustitia excedens terris vestigia fecit.

Me vero primum dulces ante omnia Musae,
quarum sacra fero ingenti percussus amore,
accipiant caelique vias et sidera monstrent,
defectus solis varios lunaeque labores;
unde tremor terris, qua vi maria alta tumescant
obicibus ruptis rursusque in se ipsa residant,
quid tantum Oceano properent se tinguere soles
hiberni, vel quae tardis mora noctibus obstet.
sin, has ne possim naturae accedere pratis,
frigidus obstiterit circum praecordia sanguis,
rura mihi et rigui placeant in vallibus amnes,
flumina amem silvasque inglorius. o ubi campi
Spercheosque et virginibus bacchata Lacaenis
Taygeta! o qui me gelidis convallibus Haemi
sistat et ingenti ramorum protegat umbra!

Felix, qui potuit rerum cognoscere causas,
atque metus omnis et inexorabile fatum
subiecit pedibus strepitumque Acherontis avari.
fortunatus et ille, deos qui novit agrestis,
Panaque Silvanumque senem Nymphasque sorores.
illum non populi fasces, non purpura regum
flexit et infidos agitans discordia fratres,
aut coniurato descendens Dacus ab Histro,

And for the gods. When Justice left the earth,
She left her footprint here, among such people.

But as for me, oh may the gracious Muses,
Gracious beyond all else, whose holy emblems
I consecrated bear in the procession,
Grant me their favor and reveal to me
The courses of the stars above in the heavens;
Teach me about the sun in its eclipse,
And about the many labors of the moon;
What is it that causes quakings of the earth?
What force is it that suddenly makes the great
Sea rise and swell and break through all restraints
And then subside into itself again?
Why is it that the sun in winter hurries
To plunge itself into the sea and why
Is the winter night so slow to come to an end?
But if the blood around my heart's too cold
To gain me access to such mighty knowledge,
Then may I find delight in the rural fields
And the little brooks that make their way through valleys,
And in obscurity love the woods and rivers.
I long for such places, oh I long to be
By Spercheus or at Táygeta in Sparta
Where maidens celebrate the rites of Bacchus,
Or to be safe in the cool Haemian glade,
Protected in the shade of those great branches!

That man is blessed who has learned the causes of things,
And therefore under his feet subjugates fear
And the decrees of unrelenting fate
And the noise of Acheron's insatiable waters.
He too is happy who knows the country gods,
The sister Nymphs, and Pan, and old Sylvanus.
He's undisturbed by worldly honors, or by
The purple worn by kings, or by the strife
Of faithless brother fighting faithless brother,
Or by the leagued barbarians from the north,
The Dacians and their allies from the Danube,

non res Romanae perituraque regna; neque ille
aut doluit miserans inopem aut invidit habenti.
quos rami fructus, quos ipsa volentia rura
sponte tulere sua, carpsit, nec ferrea iura
insanumque forum aut populi tabularia vidit.
sollicitant alii remis freta caeca, ruuntque
in ferrum, penetrant aulas et limina regum;
hic petit excidiis urbem miserosque penates,
ut gemma bibat et Sarrano dormiat ostro;
condit opes alius defossoque incubat auro;
hic stupet attonitus rostris; hunc plausus hiantem
per cuneos geminatus enim plebisque patrumque
corripuit; gaudent perfusi sanguine fratrum,
exsilioque domos et dulcia limina mutant
atque alio patriam quaerunt sub sole iacentem.
    Agricola incurvo terram dimovit aratro:
hinc anni labor, hinc patriam parvosque nepotes
sustinet, hinc armenta boum meritosque iuvencos.
nec requies, quin aut pomis exuberet annus
aut fetu pecorum aut Cerealis mergite culmi,
proventuque oneret sulcos atque horrea vincat.
venit hiems: teritur Sicyonia baca trapetis,
glande sues laeti redeunt, dant arbuta silvae;

Or by the skill of Roman power causing
Dynasties across the world to perish.
He neither looks with pity on the poor
Nor does he look with envy at the rich.
He takes from his fields and from his orchard boughs
What they have offered of their own free will,
Nor does he have experience of the iron
Hard-heartedness of the law, the Forum's madness,
Insolence of bureaucratic office.

There are those who with their oars disturb the waters
Of dangerous unknown seas, and those who rush
Against the sword, and those who insinuate
Their way into the chamber of a king;
There's the one who brings down ruin on a city
And all its wretched households, in his desire
To drink from an ornate cup and go to sleep
On Tyrian-purple coverlets at night;
There's the man who heaps up gold, and hides it away,
Hovering watchfully over it like a lover;
There's he who stares up stupefied at the Rostrum;
There's the open-mouthed undone astonishment
Of the one who hears the waves and waves of the wild
Applause of the close-packed crowd in the theater;
There are those who bathe in their brothers' blood, rejoicing;
And those who give up house and home for exile,
Seeking a land an alien sun shines on.

The farmer works the soil with his curved plow;
This is the work he does, and it sustains
His country, and his family, and his cattle,
His worthy bullocks and his herd of cows.
No rest from this, but the year will abound with fruits,
With newborn livestock, and with Ceres' sheaves
Filling the fields and overflowing the barn.
Then winter is coming: the olive press is turning;
The pigs come home well-fed, made happy by acorns;
The woods offer arbutus, and autumn yields
All its variety; high up, on the rocks,

et varios ponit fetus autumnus, et alte
mitis in apricis coquitur vindemia saxis.
interea dulces pendent circum oscula nati,
casta pudicitiam servat domus, ubera vaccae
lactea demittunt, pinguesque in gramine laeto
inter se adversis luctantur cornibus haedi.
ipse dies agitat festos fususque per herbam,
ignis ubi in medio et socii cratera coronant,
te libans, Lenaee, vocat pecorisque magistris
velocis iaculi certamina ponit in ulmo,
corporaque agresti nudant praedura palaestrae.
    Hanc olim veteres vitam coluere Sabini,
hanc Remus et frater, sic fortis Etruria crevit
scilicet et rerum facta est pulcherrima Roma,
septemque una sibi muro circumdedit arces.
ante etiam sceptrum Dictaei regis et ante
impia quam caesis gens est epulata iuvencis,
aureus hanc vitam in terris Saturnus agebat;
necdum etiam audierant inflari classica, necdum
impositos duris crepitare incudibus ensis.
    Sed nos immensum spatiis confecimus aequor,
et iam tempus equum fumantia solvere colla.

The year's vintage mellows in the sunshine.
The farmer's simple house is pure and chaste.
His children gather around him for his kisses;
On the joyful lawn the little goats fight their battles,
Butting their horns; the cows' udders are full;
It's holiday time for the farmer: at ease on the grass,
With a fire going and friends wreathing the wine bowl,
He pours a libation, Bacchus, in honor of you,
While for the game of darts some of the shepherds
Put up a target on a nearby elm,
And others of them bare their sturdy limbs,
All ready for the rustic wrestling matches.

This is what it was like for the Sabines then,
And for Romulus and Remus, in the old days.
This must be how Etruria grew strong,
And Rome became the most beautiful thing there is,
One single wall surrounding seven hills.
Indeed, before the reign began of the king
Born on the Cretan mountain, and before
Impious men first feasted on slaughtered bullocks,
This is the way it was for golden Saturn,
Before the time when anyone had heard
The loud blare of a military trumpet
Or the clanging of a sword on the hard anvil.

But now we have come a great long way and now
The time has come to unyoke our steaming horses.

THIRD GEORGIC

Te quoque, magna Pales, et te memorande canemus
pastor ab Amphryso, vos, silvae amnesque Lycaei.
cetera, quae vacuas tenuissent carmine mentes,
omnia iam vulgata: quis aut Eurysthea durum
aut inlaudati nescit Busiridis aras?
cui non dictus Hylas puer et Latonia Delos
Hippodameque umeroque Pelops insignis eburno,
acer equis? temptanda via est, qua me quoque possim
tollere humo victorque virum volitare per ora.
primus ego in patriam mecum, modo vita supersit,
Aonio rediens deducam vertice Musas;
primus Idumaeas referam tibi, Mantua, palmas
et viridi in campo templum de marmore ponam
propter aquam, tardis ingens ubi flexibus errat
Mincius et tenera praetexit harundine ripas.
in medio mihi Caesar erit templumque tenebit.
illi victor ego et Tyrio conspectus in ostro
centum quadriiugos agitabo ad flumina currus.
cuncta mihi, Alpheum linquens lucosque Molorci,

And now, great Pales, we will sing of you
And you, O famous shepherd of the Amphrýsos,
And you, O streams and forests of Lycaeus.
Those other songs, that might have brought delight
Once more to idle minds, have all been sung
So many times. Who has not heard already
The story of the harsh king Eurysthéus?
Who has not heard of cruel Busíris's altars?
So many have sung the story of Hylas lost,
Or the story of Latóna and her Delos,
Or of Hippodamía, and of ivory-shouldered
Pelops and his horses. I too must find
The way to rise in flight above the earth,
Triumphant on the speech of men, for I
Will be the first, if life be granted me,
To bring the Muses home from Helicon
To my own native country. Mantua,
I'll bring the Idumaean palms to you,
And on the green fields there beside your river—
Great Mincius slow meandering between
His banks on which the reeds profusely grow—
I'll build a temple made of Parian marble,
And Caesar will be seated in the center.

Victorious I, in Tyrian purple clad,
Will cause a hundred four-horse chariots
To course along the banks in Caesar's honor.
For me all Greece will leave Molorchus's grove
And Alpheus behind, and they will come,

cursibus et crudo decernet Graecia caestu.
ipse caput tonsae foliis ornatus olivae
dona feram. iam nunc sollemnis ducere pompas
ad delubra iuvat caesosque videre iuvencos,
vel scaena ut versis discedat frontibus utque
purpurea intexti tollant aulaea Britanni.
in foribus pugnam ex auro solidoque elephanto
Gangaridum faciam victorisque arma Quirini,
atque hic undantem bello magnumque fluentem
Nilum ac navali surgentis aere columnas.
addam urbes Asiae domitas pulsumque Niphaten
fidentemque fuga Parthum versisque sagittis
et duo rapta manu diverso ex hoste tropaea
bisque triumphatas utroque ab litore gentes.
stabunt et Parii lapides, spirantia signa,
Assaraci proles demissaeque ab Iove gentis
nomina Trosque parens et Troiae Cynthius auctor.
Invidia infelix Furias amnemque severum
Cocyti metuet tortosque Ixionis anguis
immanemque rotam et non exsuperabile saxum.
    Interea Dryadum silvas saltusque sequamur
intactos, tua, Maecenas, haud mollia iussa.
te sine nil altum mens incohat: en age, segnis

Competitors in the racing and the boxing
(Wearing our spiked and weighted Roman gloves),
And I, crowned with a wreath of olive leaves,
Will be the President of the Games, and give
The prizes to the winners. Already now
I long to see the procession as it moves
In ceremonial order to the shrine
And be a witness to the sacrifice
Of bullocks, and to see the changing scenes
As the Britons pictured on the crimson curtains
Pull on the ropes to raise those curtains up.
And on the pictured portals of the shrine
I'll show, fashioned in gold and ivory,
The battle with the Gangárides, and the arms
Of Romulus, who was deified, and show
The overflowing of the river Nile,
Billowing with warfare; and there'll be
Great columns rising high, adorned with bronze
Trophies of navies that Roman power had taken;
Images of the defeated cities of Asia;
Beaten Niphátes; Parthians launching arrows
Over their shoulders even as they flee;
Two monuments of Rome's past victories seized
From foes in faraway places in the world;
And marble statues standing all about,
Looking as if they were alive and breathing,
The children and children's children of Assarácus
And all those famous names descended from Jove
Through Tros our parent, and Cynthian Apollo,
Founder of the city that we came from.
Envy, wretched, in fear, will quail before
The Furies and the terrible river Cocýtos,
And Ixíon's frightful wheel and serpent chains,
And the unrelenting stone of Sísyphus.

Now we must go, by your command, Maecénas,
To the forests of the dryads and the glades
No one has ever trodden on before;
The way is hard; without your help my mind

rumpe moras; vocat ingenti clamore Cithaeron
Taygetique canes domitrixque Epidaurus equorum,
et vox adsensu nemorum ingeminata remugit.
mox tamen ardentis accingar dicere pugnas
Caesaris et nomen fama tot ferre per annos,
Tithoni prima quot abest ab origine Caesar.

Seu quis Olympiacae miratus praemia palmae
pascit equos, seu quis fortis ad aratra iuvencos,
corpora praecipue matrum legat. optima torvae
forma bovis, cui turpe caput, cui plurima cervix,
et crurum tenus a mento palearia pendent;
tum longo nullus lateri modus; omnia magna,
pes etiam; et camuris hirtae sub cornibus aures.
nec mihi displiceat maculis insignis et albo,
aut iuga detrectans interdumque aspera cornu
et faciem tauro propior, quaeque ardua tota
et gradiens ima verrit vestigia cauda.
aetas Lucinam iustosque pati hymenaeos
desinit ante decem, post quattuor incipit annos;
cetera nec feturae habilis nec fortis aratris.
interea, superat gregibus dum laeta iuventas,
solve mares; mitte in Venerem pecuaria primus,
atque aliam ex alia generando suffice prolem.
optima quaeque dies miseris mortalibus aevi
prima fugit; subeunt morbi tristisque senectus

Could never undertake to reach such heights.
Therefore, without delay, let us begin:
Cithaeron clamors, the Spartan hounds are barking,
And Epidáurus, tamer of horses, calls;
The sound reverberates, redoubled and
Redoubled by the woods as they applaud.
And soon I'll gird myself to tell the tales
Of Caesar's brilliant battles, and carry his name
In story across as many future years
As the years that have gone by, from the long-ago
Birth of Tithónus to that of Caesar himself.

He who breeds horses, hoping to win the prize,
Or he who breeds bullocks, to make them strong for plowing,
Whichever of these it is, had better pay
Special attention to what the mothers look like.
The best-looking cow looks fierce, with a great thick neck,
An ugly head, and dewlaps hanging down
From her jaws to her legs; extremely long in the flank;
Everything big about her, including her feet;
Her big ears shaggy under her curving horns.
Nor would I be displeased to see white markings,
Or that she is rebellious at the yoke,
With an unpredictable horn you have to watch out for.
Her expression's more like a bull's than a cow's; tall beast;
Her long tail sweeps her footprints as she walks.
The proper time for motherhood and mating
Falls between the fourth year and the tenth;
After that time she's no longer suitable,
Nor is she strong enough for the work of plowing;
But while she's in this youthful fertile time
Let the young males out, loose and free in the fields,
And be the first to see to the annual mating.
Over and over, renew your stock by breeding.

The best days of life, for all poor mortal creatures,
Are the soonest to be gone; then illness comes,

et labor, et durae rapit inclementia mortis.
semper erunt, quarum mutari corpora malis:
semper enim refice ac, ne post amissa requiras,
anteveni et subolem armento sortire quotannis.
   Nec non et pecori est idem delectus equino.
tu modo, quos in spem statues submittere gentis,
praecipuum iam inde a teneris impende laborem.
continuo pecoris generosi pullus in arvis
altius ingreditur et mollia crura reponit;
primus et ire viam et fluvios temptare minacis
audet et ignoto sese committere ponti,
nec vanos horret strepitus. illi ardua cervix
argutumque caput, brevis alvus obesaque terga,
luxuriatque toris animosum pectus. honesti
spadices glaucique, color deterrimus albis
et gilvo. tum, si qua sonum procul arma dedere,
stare loco nescit, micat auribus et tremit artus,
collectumque fremens volvit sub naribus ignem.
densa iuba, et dextro iactata recumbit in armo;
at duplex agitur per lumbos spina, cavatque
tellurem et solido graviter sonat ungula cornu.
talis Amyclaei domitus Pollucis habenis
Cyllarus et, quorum Grai meminere poetae,
Martis equi biiuges et magni currus Achilli.
talis et ipse iubam cervice effundit equina

And sad old age, and trouble; and pitiless death
Soon carries us away. There'll always be
Cows that you'll want to sell or trade because
They don't look the best for breeding, so be sure
To replace them with others, before you come to regret it;
Be sure new young are born, year after year.

The same standards apply for raising horses:
Be sure you take exceptional pains with those
That from the earliest days of their lives show signs
They'll be the best for stud. Right from the first
The foal of a superior breed will show
That he's a higher stepper than all the other
Foals there are in the fields, and puts his feet
More lightly down again on the soft turf.
He'll always be the one to lead the rest;
He'll dare to cross the threatening stream, he'll try
The bridge he never tried before, he won't
Startle or shy at an unfamiliar noise.
His neck's erect, his clean-cut head held high,
His belly tight, and his strong back is broad,
His noble chest is packed with powerful muscle.
(Chestnut and gray are best, for elegance;
White and dun are the least desirable colors.)
And if he hears a faraway sound of war,
He pricks up his flickering ears, he can't stay still,
He trembles with excitement in every limb,
Breathing out pent-up fire from snorting nostrils.
And when he tosses his head his copious mane
Falls back over and onto his right shoulder;
The spine along his loin is a double ridge;
His horn hoof strikes the earth with a ringing sound.
This is what Pollux's Cýllarus was like,
And what those horses were like, which the Greek poets
Told us about, the two yoked horses of Mars,
And great Achilles' pair; and this is what
Saturn himself was like, his thick mane flowing

coniugis adventu pernix Saturnus, et altum
Pelion hinnitu fugiens implevit acuto.
    Hunc quoque, ubi aut morbo gravis aut iam segnior annis
deficit, abde domo, nec turpi ignosce senectae.
Frigidus in Venerem senior, frustraque laborem
ingratum trahit; et, si quando ad proelia ventum est,
ut quondam in stipulis magnus sine viribus ignis,
incassum furit. ergo animos aevumque notabis
praecipue; hinc alias artes prolemque parentum,
et quis cuique dolor victo, quae gloria palmae.
nonne vides, cum praecipiti certamine campum
corripuere, ruuntque effusi carcere currus,
cum spes adrectae iuvenum, exsultantiaque haurit
corda pavor pulsans? illi instant verbere torto
et proni dant lora, volat vi fervidus axis;
iamque humiles iamque elati sublime videntur
aëra per vacuum ferri atque adsurgere in auras.
nec mora nec requies; at fulvae nimbus harenae
tollitur, umescunt spumis flatuque sequentum:
tantus amor laudum, tantae est victoria curae.
primus Ericthonius currus et quattuor ausus
iungere equos rapidusque rotis insistere victor.
frena Pelethronii Lapithae gyrosque dedere

Over his shoulders as, seeing his wife, he fled,
His whinnying heard to the top of Pelion Mountain.

Yet even such a wonderful creature as this,
When, either because of sickness or because
Of the passage of the years, he begins to become
Less than he was, you put him away in a stall,
Without regard for the shame of his old age.
When the stallion gets old he's cold in matters of love;
When he comes to that field of battle, he struggles, frustrated,
Trying to deal with his unwelcome plight;
It's as it is when in a field of stubble
A great fire rages, and rages to no avail.
So therefore be respectful of his age
And his great heart, the deeds he has performed,
The lineage of excellence he derives from,
His grief when he experiences defeat,
His joy when he has won a victory.

You've seen it, how the chariots flood out
Onto the track from the starting place, you've seen them,
Headlong in frenzied competition, all
The drivers' hearts pounding with frantic hope
Of being the first and fear of being the last,
And on and on they go, and round and round,
Lap after lap, the fiery wheels revolving,
The drivers flailing their whips, now bending low,
Stooping over the reins, now rising up—
It looks like they're carried flying up and out
Into empty air—no stopping them, no rest,
Clouds of yellow sand blown back in the eyes
Of those who follow after, the foaming breath
Of the gasping panting horses wetting the backs
Of the chariot drivers ahead, so great their love
Of glory, so great their love of victory.
Brave Erichthónius was the first to yoke
Four horses to a chariot and to stand
Triumphant up there over the whirling wheels;
The Pelethronian Lapiths were the first

impositi dorso, atque equitem docuere sub armis
insultare solo et gressus glomerare superbos.
aequus uterque labor, aeque iuvenemque magistri
exquirunt calidumque animis et cursibus acrem.
quamvis saepe fuga versos ille egerit hostis
et patriam Epirum referat fortisque Mycenas,
Neptunique ipsa deducat origine gentem.
    His animadversis instant sub tempus et omnis
impendunt curas denso distendere pingui,
quem legere ducem et pecori dixere maritum,
florentisque secant herbas fluviosque ministrant
farraque, ne blando nequeat superesse labori
invalidique patrum referant ieiunia nati.
ipsa autem macie tenuant armenta volentes,
atque, ubi concubitus primos iam nota voluptas
sollicitat, frondesque negant et fontibus arcent.
saepe etiam cursu quatiunt et sole fatigant,
cum graviter tunsis gemit area frugibus, et cum
surgentem ad Zephyrum paleae iactantur inanes.
hoc faciunt, nimio ne luxu obtunsior usus
sit genitali arvo et sulcos oblimet inertis,
sed rapiat sitiens Venerem interiusque recondat.

To mount on horseback and to bridle horses,
And train them to circle and wheel, and they were the first
To teach a man in all his armor to leap
On a horse's back and gallop across the plain
And proudly put his steed through all its paces.
The trainers want a hot-blooded lusty youth
With an eager spirit either for race or war.
Remember, though, that the other one, the old
Stallion in the stall, was he who drove
The enemy before him and claims descent
From the horses of Epírus, or brave Mycenae,
Or back through ancient days to Neptune himself.

When the mating time is soon to come around,
Great care is taken over the body of him
Who's chosen to be the master of the herd,
The lord and husband: they bring him plenty of fresh
Spring water, lots of barley, and flowering grasses
They've cut for him to keep him fat and fit
For the work of making love, and to ensure
That no weak offspring will be born who carries
The weakness of a father into the future.

But at the very same time, when in the mares
There are voluptuous familiar stirrings,
The leafy food of the mares is scanted on purpose,
In order to make them as lean as possible;
They're kept away from going to the springs;
And in the harvest season, when the floor
Shakes and groans with the threshing of the corn
And the chaff is blown about in the freshening breeze,
They gallop them a lot when the sun is hot,
To tire them out, doing this to keep
The readiness of the procreative soil
From being dulled, and its furrows clogged and sluggish,
So that the thirsty field will eagerly
Seize the entering seed and store it within.

Rursus cura patrum cadere et succedere matrum
incipit. exactis gravidae cum mensibus errant,
non illas gravibus quisquam iuga ducere plaustris,
non saltu superare viam sit passus et acri
carpere prata fuga fluviosque innare rapacis.
saltibus in vacuis pascunt et plena secundum
flumina, muscus ubi et viridissima gramine ripa,
speluncaeque tegant et saxea procubet umbra.
est lucos Silari circa ilicibusque virentem
plurimus Alburnum volitans, cui nomen asilo
Romanum est, oestrum Grai vertere vocantes,
asper, acerba sonans, quo tota exterrita silvis
diffugiunt armenta, furit mugitibus aether
concussus silvaeque et sicci ripa Tanagri.
hoc quondam monstro horribilis exercuit iras
Inachiae Iuno pestem meditata iuvencae.
hunc quoque (nam mediis fervoribus acrior instat)
arcebis gravido pecori, armentaque pasces
sole recens orto aut noctem ducentibus astris.

Post partum cura in vitulos traducitur omnis;
continuoque notas et nomina gentis inurunt,
et quos aut pecori malint submittere habendo
aut aris servare sacros aut scindere terram
et campum horrentem fractis invertere glaebis.
cetera pascuntur viridis armenta per herbas.

Then it's the turn of care for the fathers to lapse,
And the turn of care for the mothers to begin.
When the pregnant mares are wandering about
This way and that, because their time is near,
Let no one hitch them up to the heavy plow;
You have to restrain the cows from moving around
Too vigorously while grazing in the fields;
Keep them from leaping as they go; and keep them
From getting into rivers, breasting swift currents.
At this time of the year men pasture them
In quiet forest glades, alongside quiet
Rivers full to the brim, where the greenest of grass
Grows on the riverbanks, and where there's moss
For them to graze on, sheltering grottoes, and rocks
That cast long shadows over them to protect them.

In the ilex groves of Silarus and among
The green holm-oak trees of Alburnus there's
A winged insect called by men the gadfly,
Asilus in our Latin, *oestrus* in Greek;
Fierce creature, with a piercing hideous wail:
Whole herds, hysterical, hearing it, will scatter
Bellowing through the woods, the noise of their madness
Stunning the air, the trees, and Tanager's banks.
Using this frightful monster, long ago,
Was Juno's way of taking her revenge
On Ínachus of Argos's daughter, Ío.
Gadfly attacks are worst in the heat of noon;
To keep them away from your herds, graze them just after
The sun has come up in the morning or when the stars,
As they come out, are bringing on the night.

Next it's the turn of special care for the calves.
Almost as soon as the calves are born they're branded
With their own mark and the mark of the stock they belong to.
Some are selected to be raised for breeding,
Some set aside to be brought to the holy altars,
Some destined to plow the ground and churn the clods,
The rest of them left to browse in the green meadows.

tu quos ad studium atque usum formabis agrestem,
iam vitulos hortare viamque insiste domandi,
dum faciles animi iuvenum, dum mobilis aetas.
ac primum laxos tenui de vimine circlos
cervici subnecte; dehinc, ubi libera colla
servitio adsuerint, ipsis e torquibus aptos
iunge pares, et coge gradum conferre iuvencos;
atque illis iam saepe rotae ducantur inanes
per terram, et summo vestigia pulvere signent;
post valido nitens sub pondere faginus axis
instrepat, et iunctos temo trahat aereus orbis.
interea pubi indomitae non gramina tantum
nec vescas salicum frondes ulvamque palustrem,
sed frumenta manu carpes sata; nec tibi fetae
more patrum nivea implebunt mulctraria vaccae,
sed tota in dulcis consument ubera natos.

    Sin ad bella magis studium turmasque ferocis,
aut Alphea rotis praelabi flumina Pisae
et Iovis in luco currus agitare volantis:
primus equi labor est animos atque arma videre
bellantum lituosque pati, tractuque gementem
ferre rotam et stabulo frenos audire sonantis;
tum magis atque magis blandis gaudere magistri
laudibus et plausae sonitum cervicis amare.
atque haec iam primo depulsus ab ubere matris

Begin the training early for those you've chosen
To work on the farm; begin while they're still young,
Their spirits docile and easy to discipline.
First, loosely tie around their necks a circle
Of osier wands or some such pliant shoots,
And after a little while, their free necks having
Become accustomed to their servitude,
Tie the young bullocks together two by two,
Collar tethered to collar, and make them learn
To walk together, step by step, a pair;
Then have them practice pulling an empty cart
Back and forth on the place, leaving faint signs
Of the cart-wheel tracks and their own tracks on the sand;
And later on, let the straining beechwood axle
Of a loaded wagon groan as the wheels are dragged
Along the ground, pulled by a brass-bound pole.
And while they're young, and not yet broken in
To the yoke and wagon, don't feed them only on hay
Or skimpy willow leaves or sedge from the marshes;
Feed them on grain you've picked for them by hand;
And don't fill up the snowy milking-pail,
As your fathers did, withholding from her dear
Children some portion of their mother's bounty,
But let her udders yield it all to them.

But if what you have in mind for your horse, instead,
Is war and the proud fierce cavalry, or else
Racing your gliding flying chariot
Along the banks of Pisa's Alphaean waters
Or through the Olympian grove of Jupiter,
The first thing that the young foal has to learn
Is to look upon the armor of the warriors
And listen to the music of martial trumpets,
And the groaning noise, as they're pulled along, of the wheels
Of the military cars, and the jangling noise
Of halter, bit, and bridle in the stable,
Rejoicing more and more in his trainer's plaudits
And the sounds of his trainer's hands patting his neck.
And after he's weaned from his mother, let him be

audeat, inque vicem det mollibus ora capistris
invalidus etiamque tremens, etiam inscius aevi.
at tribus exactis ubi quarta accesserit aestas,
carpere mox gyrum incipiat gradibusque sonare
compositis, sinuetque alterna volumina crurum,
sitque laboranti similis; tum cursibus auras,
tum vocet, ac per aperta volans, ceu liber habenis,
aequora vix summa vestigia ponat harena:
qualis Hyperboreis Aquilo cum densus ab oris
incubuit, Scythiaeque hiemes atque arida differt
nubila; tum segetes altae campique natantes
lenibus horrescunt flabris, summaeque sonorem
dant silvae, longique urgent ad litora fluctus;
ille volat, simul arva fuga, simul aequora verrens.
hic vel ad Elei metas et maxima campi
sudabit spatia et spumas aget ore cruentas,
Belgica vel molli melius feret esseda collo.
tum demum crassa magnum farragine corpus
crescere iam domitis sinito: namque ante domandum
ingentis tollent animos, prensique negabunt
verbera lenta pati et duris parere lupatis.

 Sed non ulla magis vires industria firmat,
quam Venerem et caeci stimulos avertere amoris,
sive boum sive est cui gratior usus equorum.
atque ideo tauros procul atque in sola relegant

Persuaded, once in a while, though weak and trembling,
Not knowing yet what life is all about,
To accept a soft halter-strap in his tender mouth.
But when his fourth summer has come around, then have him
Begin to canter and gallop on the track,
And work him very hard to show him how
To put his feet down evenly as he runs,
Making a perfectly regular pattern of sounds.
And after he's mastered that, and when he's ready,
Then let him challenge the winds to race with him
As he flies across the open plains, as if
Utterly free of reins and leaving behind him
Scarcely a trace of his footsteps on the sand,
As when Áquiló the great North Wind sweeps down
From the Hyperborean coasts and scatters dry clouds
And Scythian storms before it in its way,
And the deep fields of grain and the watery lowlands
Shiver and tremble under the gentle gusts,
And rattling sounds in the high treetops are heard,
And the long waves roll in toward the waiting shore,
And the wind flies on, sweeping both land and sea.
It is such a horse as this will be the one,
Laboring toward the Olympic finish line,
Sweat-pouring and with bloody foaming mouth,
Lap after lap, around the great-race course,
Or, better still, he'll be the one whose neck
Docilely will accept the snaffle and halter
Of the chariot of war. Wait until after
The process of the breaking-in is done
Before you fatten him up with a diet of mash;
If they get too big before they're broken in,
They'll rebel against the whip or the cruel bit.

But, whether it's cattle or horses that you're rearing,
Nothing is as important for keeping them strong
As guarding them from the secret enticements of lust.
That is the reason bulls are sent away

pascua, post montem oppositum et trans flumina lata,
aut intus clausos satura ad praesepia servant.
carpit enim vires paulatim uritque videndo
femina, nec nemorum patitur meminisse nec herbae
dulcibus illa quidem inlecebris, et saepe superbos
cornibus inter se subigit decernere amantis.
pascitur in magna Sila formosa iuvenca:
illi alternantes multa vi proelia miscent
vulneribus crebris, lavit ater corpora sanguis,
versaque in obnixos urgentur cornua vasto
cum gemitu; reboant silvaeque et longus Olympus.
nec mos bellantis una stabulare, sed alter
victus abit longeque ignotis exsulat oris,
multa gemens ignominiam plagasque superbi
victoris, tum quos amisit inultus amores,
et stabula aspectans regnis excessit avitis.
ergo omni cura viris exercet et inter
dura iacet pernox instrato saxa cubili,
frondibus hirsutis et carice pastus acuta,
et temptat sese atque irasci in cornua discit
arboris obnixus trunco, ventosque lacessit
ictibus, et sparsa ad pugnam proludit harena.
post ubi collectum robur viresque refectae,
signa movet praecepsque oblitum fertur in hostem:
fluctus uti medio coepit cum albescere ponto,

To pasture all by themselves in lonely meadows
On the other side of intervening mountains,
Or across wide rivers, or else walled up alone
Inside enclosures, with their own bins for feeding.
Seeing the female enflames them, and little by little
Weakens and wastes away their vital powers.
And she, with her sweet allurements, distracts them from
Remembering their woods and quiet pastures,
And, many times, she excites two ardent suitors
To fight it out in battle with their horns.

In the Forest of Sila a beautiful heifer is grazing,
And because of her, two raging bulls contend
In violent tremendous altercation,
Charging with leveled horns, butting and goring,
The black blood flowing down their sides; their mighty
Bellowing re-echoes and re-echoes
From the woods up to the top of the nearby mountain.
Nor is it the custom for the combatants to dwell
Together after the fight; the one who has lost
Has to go elsewhere, exiled to unknown places,
Grieving over his shame and because of the blows
He suffered from the one who conquered him,
And because the loss of his love is unavenged.
With a sidelong look at the stall that was his own,
He takes his leave of his fathers' territory.
Where he has gone to he sleeps on bare hard stones
And has nothing to pasture on but bristly leaves
And pointed reed-grass, and in grief and shame
He studies how to restore and strengthen his powers.
He puts himself to the test, and in order to learn
To fill his vengeful horns with the power of fury
Charges at tree trunks, strikes blows against the winds
Again and again, and paws the sand, preparing.
Then when his strength is gathered, his powers renewed,
He carries the banner into battle, rushing
Headlong upon the unwary unready foe,
As when far out in the ocean a white froth first
Begins to show on a deep sea-surge, and then

longius ex altoque sinum trahit, utque volutus
ad terras immane sonat per saxa, neque ipso
monte minor procumbit; at ima exaestuat unda
verticibus nigramque alte subiectat harenam.

Omne adeo genus in terris hominumque ferarumque,
et genus aequoreum, pecudes pictaeque volucres,
in furias ignemque ruunt: amor omnibus idem.
tempore non alio catulorum oblita leaena
saevior erravit campis, nec funera vulgo
tam multa informes ursi stragemque dedere
per silvas; tum saevus aper, tum pessima tigris;
heu male tum Libyae solis erratur in agris.
nonne vides, ut tota tremor pertemptet equorum
corpora, si tantum notas odor attulit auras?
ac neque eos iam frena virum neque verbera saeva,
non scopuli rupesque cavae atque obiecta retardant
flumina correptosque unda torquentia montis.
ipse ruit dentesque Sabellicus exacuit sus,
et pede prosubigit terram, fricat arbore costas,
atque hinc atque illinc umeros ad vulnera durat.
quid iuvenis, magnum cui versat in ossibus ignem
durus amor? nempe abruptis turbata procellis
nocte natat caeca serus freta; quem super ingens
porta tonat caeli, et scopulis inlisa reclamant
aequora; nec miseri possunt revocare parentes,
nec moritura super crudeli funere virgo.
quid lynces Bacchi variae et genus acre luporum
atque canum? quid quae imbelles dant proelia cervi?
scilicet ante omnis furor est insignis equarum;

The sea-surge raises itself and rises and arches
And becomes a great comber rushing in toward land
And along the rocks and reefs with enormous noise,
And big as a mountain falling crashes down,
The water boiling up in violent eddies,
And from the bottom throwing black sand high.

All living creatures on earth, no matter whether
It's human beings or other kinds—fish, cattle,
Beautiful birds—they all rush into the fire:
Love is the same for all. There's no other time
When the lioness forgets her cubs and prowls
With such avid savagery across the plains;
When the shapeless bear rampaging in the woods
Is the cause of so much havoc and destruction;
It's the time when the boar is at his very fiercest,
The tigress is at her worst. Ah! not the right time
To dare to go out in deserted Libyan fields.
Haven't you seen it, your horse begins to tremble,
His whole body shivers, because he's snuffed
A hint of a familiar scent on the breeze?
The reins won't hold him back then, nor the whip,
Nor wide opposing rivers, whose rising can
Bring mountains down into their roiling waters.
And the great Sabellian boar gets himself ready,
Rubbing his sides and shoulders on a tree trunk,
Hardening them against the wounds to come,
Whetting his tusks, pawing and pawing the ground;
And what about the youth, in the black of night,
As the midnight storm bursts over his head and the huge
Doors of the heavens thunder and clang, and waves,
Colliding against the cliffs, echo the noise?
His wretched parents cannot call him back,
Nor the thought of her whose death will be the sight
Of his poor body washed up on that shore?
And what about the wild dogs and the wolves
And Bacchus's spotted lynxes, and peaceable stags
In battle with one another? Without a doubt,
Beyond all others is the madness of mares.

et mentem Venus ipsa dedit, quo tempore Glauci
Potniades malis membra absumpsere quadrigae.
illas ducit amor trans Gargara transque sonantem
Ascanium; superant montis et flumina tranant.
continuoque avidis ubi subdita flamma medullis
(vere magis, quia vere calor redit ossibus), illae
ore omnes versae in Zephyrum stant rupibus altis
exceptantque levis auras, et saepe sine ullis
coniugiis vento gravidae (mirabile dictu)
saxa per et scopulos et depressas convallis
diffugiunt, non, Eure, tuos, neque solis ad ortus,
in Borean Caurumque, aut unde nigerrimus Auster
nascitur et pluvio contristat frigore caelum.
hic demum, hippomanes vero quod nomine dicunt
pastores, lentum destillat ab inguine virus,
hippomanes, quod saepe malae legere novercae
miscueruntque herbas et non innoxia verba.
    Sed fugit interea, fugit inreparabile tempus,
singula dum capti circumvectamur amore.
hoc satis armentis: superat pars altera curae,
lanigeros agitare greges hirtasque capellas.
hic labor, hinc laudem fortes sperate coloni.
nec sum animi dubius, verbis ea vincere magnum
quam sit et angustis hunc addere rebus honorem:
sed me Parnasi deserta per ardua dulcis
raptat amor; iuvat ire iugis, qua nulla priorum

(Venus, the goddess of love, created this madness,
At the time she caused the Potnian racing mares
To turn on their master, Glaucus, eating his limbs.)
Love drives the maddened mares to swim wide rivers;
Love drives them to climb up mountains; love drives them through
The roaring waters of Ascánius
And up the sides of Gárgara. In spring,
For it's in spring that they're in heat of love
That's burning in the marrow of their bones,
They make their way to the top of some high cliff
And stand together there, facing the west,
And snuffle the wind. And then, *mirabile dictu*,
Pregnant, but from no lover but the wind,
Over rocks and valleys and cliffs they race away,
Not, East Wind, toward the place where you arise
Nor where the sun comes up, but to the north,
Toward Boreas and Caurus, or to the south,
Where blackest Auster takes its origin,
Bringing on gloomy skies and chilling rain,
And there, and then, they stand, and from their groins
The slow slime drips that herdsmen call "horse madness"—
Hippomunes—that wicked stepmothers gather
Sometimes to mix with herbs to make their spells.

But meanwhile unrecoverable time
Is flying, flying past us while we linger,
Enraptured by our theme. Now it is time
To turn away from the herds and undertake
My other task, the care of my woolly flock
And shaggy goats. The task is hard, and so,
You sturdy shepherds, the fame would be hard won
And well deserved. Nor am I ignorant
Of the magnitude of the work of conquering
A theme like this with words, and winning glory
When the subject is so lowly. By sweet love urged
To roam Parnassus's lonely heights, it is
A delight to go where none has gone before,

Castaliam molli devertitur orbita clivo.
nunc, veneranda Pales, magno nunc ore sonandum.
　　Incipiens stabulis edico in mollibus herbam
carpere ovis, dum mox frondosa reducitur aestas,
et multa duram stipula filicumque maniplis
sternere subter humum, glacies ne frigida laedat
molle pecus scabiemque ferat turpisque podagras.
post hinc digressus iubeo frondentia capris
arbuta sufficere et fluvios praebere recentis,
et stabula a ventis hiberno opponere soli
ad medium conversa diem, cum frigidus olim
iam cadit extremoque inrorat Aquarius anno.
hae quoque non cura nobis leviore tuendae,
nec minor usus erit, quamvis Milesia magno
vellera mutentur Tyrios incocta rubores.
densior hinc suboles, hinc largi copia lactis;
quam magis exhausto spumaverit ubere mulctra,
laeta magis pressis manabunt flumina mammis.
nec minus interea barbas incanaque menta
Cinyphii tondent hirci saetasque comantis
usum in castrorum et miseris velamina nautis.
pascuntur vero silvas et summa Lycaei,
horrentisque rubos et amantis ardua dumos;
atque ipsae memores redeunt in tecta suosque
ducunt et gravido superant vix ubere limen.
ergo omni studio glaciem ventosque nivalis,
quo minor est illis curae mortalis egestas,

No predecessor's wheel track to be seen
Upon the slope down toward the Castalian spring.
O venerated Pales, now we must
Take up the theme in a sonorous lofty strain.

First, I command that you spread upon the hard
Cold ground of the pens in which you shelter your sheep
To feed on herbage over the winter, till leafy
Summer comes back, with straw and handfuls of fronds
To protect the feet of your vulnerable flock
From the ice that brings on scab and the loathsome foot-gout.
And next, I command that your goats be given plenty
Of leaves of arbutus to eat and lots of fresh water;
And that you set up stalls for them facing south,
Facing the sun, sheltered from wind, until,
At the end of winter, cold Aquarius
The Water Carrier departs in showers.

And goats deserve no less than sheep deserve;
What they provide's no less than sheep provide.
A Miletian fleece dyed with Tyrian purple
Will, to be sure, be sold for more, and yet
The nanny goats produce more offspring and
More milk; the more the milk from the udders richly
Foams in the milking-pail, the more it richly
Flows from the pressed teats at the next milking.
The billy goats' gray beards and bristly coats
Are clipped to make rough cloth for army camps
And jackets for shivering sailors against the cold.
When spring comes round again the goats are able
To forage in woods and on the Lycaean heights,
Feeding on brambles and mountain-loving briar;
And they know the way to come home all by themselves
With their kids following after, the she-goats' udders
So full that they can scarcely clear the threshold.
The more they get along without your help,
The more they need the help that you can give them,
Sheltering them from the wind and from the cold,

avertes, victumque feres et virgea laetus
pabula, nec tota claudes faenilia bruma.
    At vero Zephyris cum laeta vocantibus aestas
in saltus utrumque gregem atque in pascua mittet,
Luciferi primo cum sidere frigida rura
carpamus, dum mane novum, dum gramina canent,
et ros in tenera pecori gratissimus herba.
inde ubi quarta sitim caeli collegerit hora
et cantu querulae rumpent arbusta cicadae,
ad puteos aut alta greges ad stagna iubebo
currentem ilignis potare canalibus undam;
aestibus at mediis umbrosam exquirere vallem,
sicubi magna Iovis antiquo robore quercus
ingentis tendat ramos, aut sicubi nigrum
ilicibus crebris sacra nemus accubet umbra;
tum tenuis dare rursus aquas et pascere rursus
solis ad occasum, cum frigidus aëra vesper
temperat, et saltus reficit iam roscida luna,
litoraque alcyonem resonant, acalanthida dumi.
    Quid tibi pastores Libyae, quid pascua versu
prosequar et raris habitata mapalia tectis?
saepe diem noctemque et totum ex ordine mensem
pascitur itque pecus longa in deserta sine ullis
hospitiis: tantum campi iacet. omnia secum
armentarius Afer agit, tectumque laremque

Bringing them twigs to eat for sustenance,
And leaving your hay bins open all winter long.

But let us eagerly go now, seeking the cool
Fields where joyful summer, called to do so
By zephyrs in the early morning, sends
The sheep and goats out to the glades and pastures,
When the first star, Lucifer, appears, and the day
Is new, and the fields are hoary because of the dew
That clinging to the tender grass is most
Pleasing to the flocks; then, later in the morning,
When everywhere the querulous cicadas
Complain in every bush, and the flocks are thirsty,
I'll take them down to drink from brooks or pools,
Or the wells where water runs through oaken channels,
To quench their thirst; and after that, at noon,
When the day is at its hottest, seek out with them
Somewhere some shady place where Jove's great oak
Spreads out its giant arms from its ancient trunk,
Or a grove that lies in a holy darkness caused
By the congregated shade of ilex trees;
Then lead them in the afternoon back down
To drink from those pure murmuring trickling waters;
And pasture them again till sunset comes,
When Vesper, the evening star arising, brings
Its coolness to the air, and the dew that falls
From the risen moon refreshes the waiting glades,
And the halcyon bird is heard along the shores,
And finches in the trees and all the thickets.

How shall I tell of the Libyan shepherds, and
Their scattered settlements of little huts
Out on the vast sparse reaches of the desert,
And their flocks that wander browsing, night and day,
For months at a time, unsheltered and unfenced?
The herdsman brings his house and all that's in it,
Every last thing he owns, along with him,

armaque Amyclaeumque canem Cressamque pharetram;
non secus ac patriis acer Romanus in armis
iniusto sub fasce viam cum carpit, et hosti
ante exspectatum positis stat in agmine castris.
  At non, qua Scythiae gentes Maeotiaque unda,
turbidus et torquens flaventis Hister harenas,
quaque redit medium Rhodope porrecta sub axem.
illic clausa tenent stabulis armenta, neque ullae
aut herbae campo apparent aut arbore frondes;
sed iacet aggeribus niveis informis et alto
terra gelu late septemque adsurgit in ulnas.
semper hiems, semper spirantes frigora Cauri.
tum Sol pallentis haud umquam discutit umbras,
nec cum invectus equis altum petit aethera, nec cum
praecipitem Oceani rubro lavit aequore currum.
concrescunt subitae currenti in flumine crustae,
undaque iam tergo ferratos sustinet orbes,
puppibus illa prius, patulis nunc hospita plaustris;
aeraque dissiliunt vulgo, vestesque rigescunt
indutae, caeduntque securibus umida vina,
et totae solidam in glaciem vertere lacunae,
stiriaque impexis induruit horrida barbis.
interea toto non setius aëre ninguit:
intereunt pecudes, stant circumfusa pruinis
corpora magna boum, confertoque agmine cervi
torpent mole nova et summis vix cornibus exstant.
hos non immissis canibus, non cassibus ullis
puniceaeve agitant pavidos formidine pinnae,
sed frustra oppositum trudentis pectore montem
comminus obtruncant ferro, graviterque rudentis

And his Cretan bow and arrow, his Spartan dog,
Just as the fierce campaigning Roman soldier,
Wearing his heavy armor, halts his platoon,
Lays down his heavy pack, to pitch his tent,
In expectation of the next day's battle,
When he will attack the enemy by surprise.

It's very different up where the Scythians are,
Where the violent Danube roils its yellow sands
And the Rhodopean mountain range leans back
And reaches up, high to the central pole.
The Scythians keep their herds pent up in stalls;
The trees are leafless, terrain utterly grassless,
And everywhere the earth lies under shapeless
Piles of snow and ice seven cubits high;
It's always winter; the cold wind always blows;
The sun never dispels the icy mists,
Not when at noon he's carried by his horses
Up to the highest sky, nor when his chariot
Plunges back down into the crimson sea.
Ice without warning gathers and thickens up
Over the moving waters of the river,
And soon the stream, once welcoming to boats,
Will bear big wagons with their iron wheels
Upon its frozen surface; everywhere
Brass pipes split and burst open; the very clothes
On people's backs are frozen stiff as boards;
They have to use hatchets to get at wine to drink;
Whole lakes turn into solid blocks; icicles
Form and hang on the unkempt beards of men.
Meanwhile the storm goes on and on and fills
The sky with snow, and many cattle perish;
The oxen stand bewildered, their giant bodies
Covered with shrouds of frost; and, crowded together,
The deer are paralyzed with fright, their horns
Are barely to be seen above the drifts;
Men hunt them, not by setting loose their dogs,
Putting out nets or ropes of bright red feathers
With which to entrap them, but as the creatures vainly

caedunt, et magno laeti clamore reportant.
ipsi in defossis specubus secura sub alta
otia agunt terra, congestaque robora, totasque
advolvere focis ulmos, ignique dedere.
hic noctem ludo ducunt, et pocula laeti
fermento atque acidis imitantur vitea sorbis.
talis Hyperboreo septem subiecta trioni
gens effrena virum Riphaeo tunditur Euro
et pecudum fulvis velatur corpora saetis.

    Si tibi lanitium curae, primum aspera silva
lappaeque tribolique absint; fuge pabula laeta,
continuoque greges villis lege mollibus albos.
illum autem, quamvis aries sit candidus ipse,
nigra subest udo tantum cui lingua palato,
reice, ne maculis infuscet vellera pullis
nascentum, plenoque alium circumspice campo.
munere sic niveo lanae, si credere dignum est,
Pan deus Arcadiae captam te, Luna, fefellit
in nemora alta vocans; nec tu aspernata vocantem.

    At cui lactis amor, cytisum lotosque frequentis
ipse manu salsasque ferat praesepibus herbas:
hinc et amant fluvios magis, et magis ubera tendunt
et salis occultum referunt in lacte saporem.

Struggle to breast the mountainous white snow
The men come in with their knives and at close quarters
Butcher them as they fall, bellowing, down,
And bear the bodies away with cries of joy.
And the people themselves live comfortable and easy,
Safe and sound together in the caves
They've dug out under the earth, rolling great logs
To the blazing hearth and throwing them on the fire
And whiling the night away with joyful games,
And celebrating, instead of with wine, with beer
Or their strong drink that's made of fermented berries.
These are the Far North Hyperborean people
Living under the seven stars of the Wagon
And buffeted by the wind that blows down from
The high Riphaean crags, a race of wild men
Wearing the clothes they'd made from the skins of beasts.

If raising sheep for wool is your concern,
Be sure to avoid pasturing where the grass
Grows high, and you must keep your pasture clear
Of caltrops, burrs, and other bristling growth.
From the beginning be sure to choose for your flock
Only those sheep whose fleece is soft and white;
But no matter how white the ram, if there are veins
Of black on the underside of his moist tongue,
Reject that ram and look for another one,
So that the newborn lambs won't be dark-spotted.
O Moon, it was with a lure of pure white wool
That you, if what we're told as true is true,
Were captivated by Pan, Arcadia's god,
Calling you to the innermost forest glade,
And, so it is said, you did not spurn his call.

But he whose care is milk must be sure to carry
Lotus and medick and other salty greens
To the goats in the stalls, so that all the more they'll love
To drink from the streams and therefore all the more

multi etiam excretos prohibent a matribus haedos,
primaque ferratis praefigunt ora capistris.
quod surgente die mulsere horisque diurnis,
nocte premunt; quod iam tenebris et sole cadente,
sub lucem: exportant calathis (adit oppida pastor),
aut parco sale contingunt hiemique reponunt.

    Nec tibi cura canum fuerit postrema, sed una
velocis Spartae catulos acremque Molossum
pasce sero pingui. numquam custodibus illis
nocturnum stabulis furem incursusque luporum
aut impacatos a tergo horrebis Hiberos.
saepe etiam cursu timidos agitabis onagros,
et canibus leporem, canibus venabere dammas;
saepe volutabris pulsos silvestribus apros
latratu turbabis agens, montisque per altos
ingentem clamore premes ad retia cervum.

    Disce et odoratam stabulis accendere cedrum,
galbaneoque agitare gravis nidore chelydros.
saepe sub immotis praesepibus aut mala tactu
vipera delituit caelumque exterrita fugit,
aut tecto adsuetus coluber succedere et umbrae
(pestis acerba boum) pecorique adspergere virus,
fovit humum. cape saxa manu, cape robora, pastor,
tollentemque minas et sibila colla tumentem
deice. iamque fuga timidum caput abdidit alte,
cum medii nexus extremaeque agmina caudae

Distend their udders, and so their milk will retain
A faint savor of salt. It's the practice of many
Goatkeepers to keep the kids away from the mothers
As soon as they possibly can after they're born;
They muzzle the mouths of the kids with iron muzzles.
The milk that's yielded at dawn or in the daylight
Is pressed into cheese at night; the yield of the milking
At sunset or in the nighttime is pressed at dawn.
A shepherd with a basket carries the cheese
To town to sell at the market, or maybe they salt it
To keep it for themselves for when winter comes.

Nor should you forget the proper care of dogs.
Your Spartan dogs, so good at running, and
Your Molossians, so fierce, feed them alike
On a rich diet of whey. You'll never have to
Live with the dread of wolves getting in to your flock,
Or the nocturnal thief getting in to your stables,
Or the vagabond Spanish brigand invading your place.
How many times along with your dogs you'll pursue
The timid wild ass; how many times you'll hunt
The hare with them, and the doe; how many times
You'll rouse the wild boar out of his hidden lair
With your barking dogs, and with their noisy clamor
You'll chase the panicking roebuck over the hills
Until you run him at last into the nets.

It's important that you fumigate your stables
With the smoke of odorous cedar and Syrian gums,
To keep the filthy water snakes away.
The viper, which is fatal to the touch,
Fearful of daylight, hides out sometimes under
Stalls that have been neglected; sometimes an adder,
Which is a plague of cattle, shedder of venom,
From his hiding place up in the sheltering thatch
Has glided down and hugged the earth below.
Shepherd, pick up a stick, pick up a stone,
And strike him down as he raises his menacing head
And swells his hissing neck. Look how in flight

solvuntur, tardosque trahit sinus ultimus orbis.
est etiam ille malus Calabris in saltibus anguis,
squamea convolvens sublato pectore terga
atque notis longam maculosus grandibus alvum,
qui, dum amnes ulli rumpuntur fontibus et dum
vere madent udo terrae ac pluvialibus Austris,
stagna colit, ripisque habitans hic piscibus atram
improbus ingluviem ranisque loquacibus explet;
postquam exusta palus, terraeque ardore dehiscunt,
exsilit in siccum, et flammantia lumina torquens
saevit agris asperque siti atque exterritus aestu.
ne mihi tum mollis sub divo carpere somnos
neu dorso nemoris libeat iacuisse per herbas,
cum positis novus exuviis nitidusque iuventa
volvitur, aut catulos tectis aut ova relinquens,
arduus ad solem, et linguis micat ore trisulcis.

    Morborum quoque te causas et signa docebo.
turpis ovis temptat scabies, ubi frigidus imber
altius ad vivum persedit et horrida cano
bruma gelu, vel cum tonsis inlotus adhaesit
sudor, et hirsuti secuerunt corpora vepres.
dulcibus idcirco fluviis pecus omne magistri
perfundunt, udisque aries in gurgite villis
mersatur, missusque secundo defluit amni;

His terrified head first disappears in the ground
And then his writhing middle coils and uncoils
And the rest of him writhing straightens and follows after,
The final fold unfolding the last to vanish.
And there's that dreadful snake whose habitat
Is the marshy glades of Calabria down there,
Big-spotted along his endless underlength,
His threatening breast held high, his scaly back
Wreathing and coiling. As long as there's water gushing
Out of the sources of streams, as long as spring
And the south winds bringing their springtime rainfall steep
The earth in water, this serpent inhabits the sides
Of pools where he can satisfy his black
Throat's appetite with fish and croaking frogs.
But when the swamp is all dried out, and the soil
Is gaping wide, with rolling flaming eyes
He moves into the fields and rages frenzied,
Gone mad with hunger and thirst and because of the heat.
Keep me from giving in to the soft temptation
Of sleeping at midday under the open sky,
Or taking my ease on a slope nearby a grove,
When he comes gliding toward me through the grass,
Youthful and shining, his old skin sloughed away,
Abandoning his children in their nest,
His crest erect, darting his three-forked tongue.

I will teach you, too, about the sicknesses
That animals are afflicted with. Disgusting
Scabies attacks the sheep when cold and rain
Persist and penetrate to the quick, and all
The world is hoary with frost, or when the sweat
Hasn't been washed away after the shearing
And the sheep have wandered into the brambles and gotten
Open cuts on their vulnerable flesh.
That is the reason the shepherds lead all of their flock
Into a river to bathe, letting the ram
Float off in his soaking fleece downstream with the current.

aut tonsum tristi contingunt corpus amurca,
et spumas miscent argenti et sulpura viva
Idaeasque pices et pinguis unguine ceras
scillamque elleborosque gravis nigrumque bitumen.
non tamen ulla magis praesens fortuna laborum est,
quam si quis ferro potuit rescindere summum
ulceris os: alitur vitium vivitque tegendo,
dum medicas adhibere manus ad vulnera pastor
abnegat, et meliora deos sedet omina poscens.
quin etiam, ima dolor balantum lapsus ad ossa
cum furit atque artus depascitur arida febris,
profuit incensos aestus avertere et inter
ima ferire pedis salientem sanguine venam,
Bisaltae quo more solent acerque Gelonus,
cum fugit in Rhodopen atque in deserta Getarum,
et lac concretum cum sanguine potat equino.
quam procul aut molli succedere saepius umbrae
videris, aut summas carpentem ignavius herbas
extremamque sequi, aut medio procumbere campo
pascentem, et serae solam decedere nocti,
continuo culpam ferro compesce, prius quam
dira per incautum serpant contagia vulgus.
non tam creber agens hiemem ruit aequore turbo,
quam multae pecudum pestes. nec singula morbi
corpora corripiunt, sed tota aestiva repente,
spemque gregemque simul cunctamque ab origine gentem.

Or maybe they smear the shorn bodies with bitter
Oil of olive lees, and black bitumen, squill,
And hellebore, and silver-scum, and sulfur,
In a thick blend with pitch of Ida, and wax.

But nothing is more timely than if you're able
To bring yourself to use a knife to open
The ulcer to exposure—the ulcer grows
And nourishes itself by hiding within,
While the shepherd who isn't willing to put his hand
Healingly on the sores sits passively by
And prays to the gods to send more fortunate signs.
And furthermore, and still more urgent, if
The pain has glided its way into the very
Marrow of the bleating sick one's bones,
And rages there, and the fever is in the joints,
You should try to turn the fiery heat aside
By cutting open a vein in the creature's foot,
Letting the blood gush out; this is the practice
Among the Thracian herdsmen and the fierce
Gelónians when they migrate up to the heights
Of the Rhodopean range, or out in the wild
Desert of the Getae, they who slake their thirst
With milk that's curdled with the blood of horses.

If you should happen to notice that one of your herd
Often withdraws by itself to seek the shade,
Or, lagging behind the rest, listlessly crops
Only the tops of the grass, or sinks down sometimes,
Out in midfield, while grazing, or, long before nightfall,
As if it were nightfall, wanders away toward home,
Take action with your knife without delay,
Before the dire contagion snakes its way
All through the oblivious herd. A cyclone driving
Violent winds before it in from the sea
Is not so swift as the onslaught of the plague
Suddenly swarming down on the animals,
Not just one sick, but all of them all at once,
The flock and the hope of the flock, every last one.

tum sciat, aërias Alpis et Norica si quis
castella in tumulis et Iapydis arva Timavi
nunc quoque post tanto videat, desertaque regna
pastorum et longe saltus lateque vacantis.

Hic quondam morbo caeli miseranda coorta est
tempestas totoque autumni incanduit aestu,
et genus omne neci pecudum dedit, omne ferarum,
corrupitque lacus, infecit pabula tabo.
nec via mortis erat simplex; sed ubi ignea venis
omnibus acta sitis miseros adduxerat artus,
rursus abundabat fluidus liquor omniaque in se
ossa minutatim morbo conlapsa trahebat.
saepe in honore deum medio stans hostia ad aram,
lanea dum nivea circumdatur infula vitta,
inter cunctantis cecidit moribunda ministros.
aut si quam ferro mactaverat ante sacerdos,
inde neque impositis ardent altaria fibris,
nec responsa potest consultus reddere vates,
ac vix suppositi tinguntur sanguine cultri
summaque ieiuna sanie infuscatur harena.
hinc laetis vituli vulgo moriuntur in herbis
et dulcis animas plena ad praesepia reddunt;
hinc canibus blandis rabies venit, et quatit aegros
tussis anhela sues ac faucibus angit obesis.
labitur infelix studiorum atque immemor herbae
victor equus fontisque avertitur et pede terram
crebra ferit; demissae aures, incertus ibidem
sudor et ille quidem morituris frigidus; aret

Long after the time when it happened you can see
The effects of it, up on the Alpine slopes
Or around the forts that guarded the Nórican hills
Or where Timávus flows: pastures deserted,
The shepherds' glades all empty, far and wide.
There in that land, one year, from a morbid sky
There came a wretched autumn glowing with heat,
And every animal died, whether tame or wild;
The lakes were all infected, the pastures poisoned.
Nor was the manner of dying a simple matter:
After the thirsty slake-seeking fever had gone
All through the veins and withered the pitiful limbs,
Then a fluid welled up in the suffering body, and
Piece by piece absorbed the melting bones.
It happened sometimes that the designated
Sacrificial victim, standing beside
The altar at the moment when the priest
Was wreathing its brow with the snow-white woolen fillet,
Fell down and died before it could be slain.
Or if the priest had already used his knife
And placed the victim's entrails on the altar
They didn't burn at all; the oracle,
When called upon, had no response to give;
There was hardly any blood on the ritual knife;
On the surface of the sand under the altar
There was only the slightest stain of the watery gore.

Then everywhere in the joyous burgeoning fields
The young cows die, or in their pens, in the very
Presence of their mangers full of food,
Give up sweet life; fawning dogs go mad;
The sick swine seized with retching coughing choke
On their own swollen throats; the horse that was once
Victorious now miserably sinks
As he tries to arise, forgetting what he had been,
Forgetting his pasture with its lush green grass,
Averting his face from the waters of the trough,
Over and over again pounding the earth
With a disconsolate hoof, his ears laid back,

pellis et ad tactum tractanti dura resistit.
haec ante exitium primis dant signa diebus;
sin in processu coepit crudescere morbus,
tum vero ardentes oculi atque attractus ab alto
spiritus, interdum gemitu gravis, imaque longo
ilia singultu tendunt, it naribus ater
sanguis, et obsessas fauces premit aspera lingua.
profuit inserto latices infundere cornu
Lenaeos; ea visa salus morientibus una:
mox erat hoc ipsum exitio, furiisque refecti
ardebant, ipsique suos iam morte sub aegra
(di meliora piis erroremque hostibus illum!)
discissos nudis laniabant dentibus artus.

    Ecce autem duro fumans sub vomere taurus
concidit et mixtum spumis vomit ore cruorem
extremosque ciet gemitus. it tristis arator,
maerentem abiungens fraterna morte iuvencum,
atque opere in medio defixa relinquit aratra.
non umbrae altorum nemorum, non mollia possunt
prata movere animum, non qui per saxa volutus
purior electro campum petit amnis; at ima
solvuntur latera, atque oculos stupor urget inertis
ad terramque fluit devexo pondere cervix.
quid labor aut benefacta iuvant? quid vomere terras
invertisse gravis? atqui non Massica Bacchi
munera, non illis epulae nocuere repostae:
frondibus et victu pascuntur simplicis herbae,

Fitfully sweating; the sweat turns cold as death
As death draws near; his skin is dry and hard,
Insensible to the touch of the stroking hand.
These are the signs you witness in the first
Days of the coming on of death, but as
The suffering moves into its final phase,
His eyes glare bright with the brightness of the fever,
The horse's groaning breathing drags itself forth
From deep inside, and the whole length of the body
Labors and strains with drawn-out shuddering sobbing;
Black blood pours out of the nose, and the creature's throat
Is utterly blocked up and choked by its tongue.
There are those who've thought the only possible hope
Was to use a funnel to pour in a little wine;
But this itself facilitated death:
Revived they raged, with weird new desperate strength,
And in the final crisis (God grant such madness
Not to ourselves but to our enemies)
They tore at their own flesh with their own bared teeth.

And, pulling the heavy plowshare along the furrows,
Sweating under the weight, an ox falls dying,
Its body heaving and groaning, the blood and foam
Issuing from its mouth. The mournful plowman
Unyokes the other ox, its sorrowing brother,
Leaving the task half finished, the plowshare stilled.
The heart of the dying ox cannot be moved
By the grove's deep shadows or by the pasture's softness
Or by the purer than amber streams that make
Their way over the stones downhill to the valley.
His skin hangs loose upon his sides; inertia
Weighs heavy in the stupor of his eyes;
His heavy neck sinks heavily to the earth.
What was the use of all the work he did?
What good was it that he turned the heavy earth
With the plowshare he was yoked to? No wine of Bacchus
Brought harm to him or to the others like him;
For them there were no lavish banquets; for them
Their feast was pasture grass; their drinking cups

pocula sunt fontes liquidi atque exercita cursu
flumina, nec somnos abrumpit cura salubris.
   Tempore non alio dicunt regionibus illis
quaesitas ad sacra boves Iunonis et uris
imparibus ductos alta ad donaria currus.
ergo aegre rastris terram rimantur, et ipsis
unguibus infodiunt fruges, montisque per altos
contenta cervice trahunt stridentia plaustra.
non lupus insidias explorat ovilia circum
nec gregibus nocturnus obambulat; acrior illum
cura domat. timidi dammae cervique fugaces
nunc interque canes et circum tecta vagantur.
iam maris immensi prolem et genus omne natantum
litore in extremo ceu naufraga corpora fluctus
proluit; insolitae fugiunt in flumina phocae.
interit et curvis frustra defensa latebris
vipera et attoniti squamis astantibus hydri.
ipsis est aër avibus non aequus, et illae
praecipites alta vitam sub nube relinquunt.
praeterea iam nec mutari pabula refert,
quaesitaeque nocent artes; cessere magistri,
Phillyrides Chiron Amythaoniusque Melampus.
saevit et in lucem Stygiis emissa tenebris
pallida Tisiphone Morbos agit ante Metumque
inque dies avidum surgens caput altius effert.
balatu pecorum et crebris mugitibus amnes
arentesque sonant ripae collesque supini.

Were flowing streams or the clear water of springs;
No care disturbed their peaceful sleep at night.

At that time, there, they say, men looked for cattle
To sacrifice in the rituals of Juno,
And there were nowhere any to be found.
Ill-matched wild oxen had to be used to pull
The chariots up to the goddess's mountain temple;
And men had to scratch at the earth by themselves with harrows,
And use their own fingernails to dig the holes
To plant their seeds in, and their own strained necks
To drag their creaking wagons up the hills.
No treacherous wolf then reconnoitered the sheepfold
Nor prowled nocturnally around the flock;
His own acute distress had made him tame;
And timid does and shy elusive stags
Wandered in public where there are dogs and houses;
And there were many creatures of the deep
Whose corpses lay on beaches like the bodies
Of shipwrecked sailors washed up by the waves;
And sea calves fled from the sea to freshwater rivers;
And the viper perished, having vainly wound
Into its winding hiding-place to hide;
And the hydra too, its astonished scales erect.
Nor was the air hospitable to birds:
Falling they left their lives up under the clouds.
Nor were there remedies that made things better;
The knowledge of those who study remedies,
Like Chiron, the son of Phillýra, or Melampus,
The son of Amytháon, only did harm.

Let up into the light from the Stygian shadows
Pale Tisíphoné rages, driving on
Terror and Plague before her and every day
Raising up higher and higher her greedy head.
The lowing of the cattle and bleating of sheep
Is endlessly echoed back from waterless rivers,

iamque catervatim dat stragem atque aggerat ipsis
in stabulis turpi dilapsa cadavera tabo,
donec humo tegere ac foveis abscondere discunt.
nam neque erat coriis usus, nec viscera quisquam
aut undis abolere potest aut vincere flamma.
ne tondere quidem morbo inluvieque peresa
vellera nec telas possunt attingere putris:
verum etiam invisos si quis temptarat amictus,
ardentes papulae atque immundus olentia sudor
membra sequebatur, nec longo deinde moranti
tempore contactos artus sacer ignis edebat.

Dry banks, and supine hills. And now she brings
Death to the many and heaps up in the stables
Disgusting rotting deliquescent bodies,
Until men have to learn to dig out pits
And cover the bodies over and out of sight,
For the hides could never be put to use, nor could
They ever disinfect the meat by boiling.
They couldn't even shear the wool and use it,
It was so filthy and so full of the sickness;
The cloth would hang untouchable on the loom.
If any man should make a garment of it,
Vile sweat and fever blisters would move across
His stinking body, and pretty soon the anthrax,
Ignis sacer, would have its way with him.

FOURTH GEORGIC

Protinus aërii mellis caelestia dona
exsequar. hanc etiam, Maecenas, aspice partem.
admiranda tibi levium spectacula rerum
magnanimosque duces totiusque ordine gentis
mores et studia et populos et proelia dicam.
in tenui labor; at tenuis non gloria, si quem
numina laeva sinunt auditque vocatus Apollo.
    Principio sedes apibus statioque petenda,
quo neque sit ventis aditus (nam pabula venti
ferre domum prohibent) neque oves haedique petulci
floribus insultent, aut errans bucula campo
decutiat rorem et surgentis atterat herbas.
absint et picti squalentia terga lacerti
pinguibus a stabulis, meropesque aliaeque volucres
et manibus Procne pectus signata cruentis:
omnia nam late vastant ipsasque volantis
ore ferunt dulcem nidis immitibus escam.
at liquidi fontes et stagna virentia musco

Now, in its turn, I will pursue the subject
Of honey, heaven-sent, a gift from the sky.
Maecénas, look with favor on this story,
Which tells about a marvelous tiny scene,
And I'll in order speak of magnanimous captains,
And of an entire nation, its character,
Activities, its tribes, and of their battles.
The task is small but not the glory, if
The powers that might oppose it will allow it,
And if Apollo listens to my prayer.

First of all, find a protected place for the bees
To make their home, a place that's safe from the wind
That might prevent them from getting back with their food
And safe from the sheep or the wanton kids that trample
The flowers down, or the wandering heifer shaking
The dew from the grass and bruising the rising blades.
Protect the rich stalls of their honeycombs from the scaly
Shiny-backed lizard, and from the bee-eater and other
Birds of the sort, and Procne, whose bloody hands
Have left their signs upon her crimson breast.
Any of these can devastate the bees,
Catching them in their mouths to carry them home
As delicacies to feed to their cruel children.

And there should be a limpid spring nearby,
Or a moss-edged pool, or else a little brook,

adsint et tenuis fugiens per gramina rivus,
palmaque vestibulum aut ingens oleaster inumbret,
ut, cum prima novi ducent examina reges
vere suo, ludetque favis emissa iuventus,
vicina invitet decedere ripa calori,
obviaque hospitiis teneat frondentibus arbos.
in medium, seu stabit iners seu profluet umor,
transversas salices et grandia conice saxa,
pontibus ut crebris possint consistere et alas
pandere ad aestivum solem, si forte morantis
sparserit aut praeceps Neptuno immerserit Eurus.
haec circum casiae virides et olentia late
serpylla et graviter spirantis copia thymbrae
floreat, inriguumque bibant violaria fontem.

Ipsa autem, seu corticibus tibi suta cavatis
seu lento fuerint alvaria vimine texta,
angustos habeant aditus: nam frigore mella
cogit hiems, eademque calor liquefacta remittit.
utraque vis apibus pariter metuenda; neque illae
nequiquam in tectis certatim tenuia cera
spiramenta linunt, fucoque et floribus oras
explent, collectumque haec ipsa ad munera gluten
et visco et Phrygiae servant pice lentius Idae.
saepe etiam effossis, si vera est fama, latebris
sub terra fovere larem, penitusque repertae
pumicibusque cavis exesaeque arboris antro.
tu tamen et levi rimosa cubilia limo
ungue fovens circum, et raras superinice frondes.

Almost unseen, making its way through the grass,
And a big palm tree or oleaster shading
The vestibule of the place where the bees have settled,
So when the kings of the hive lead the swarm forth
In the welcoming season, and glad to be free at last,
The youthful bees are capering and playing,
There'll be a stream bank or a pond bank there,
Where they can escape the unaccustomed heat
And where the leaves of a tree can shelter them.
And whether it's pools or running streams, there must
Be willow shoots and stones disposed across,
As resting places for them to spread their wings
And dry them in the sun, if any had happened
To linger and were caught in a sudden shower,
Or the wind had suddenly blown them into the water.
And there should be sweet blooming marjoram near,
And the odor of serpylla spreading far,
And aromatic thyme, and violet beds
Drinking from the trickling spring or stream.

Whether the hive is made by sewing together
Concave strips of bark, or woven of pliant
Osier wands, be sure the entrance is narrow,
For winter cold makes the honey freeze and congeal,
Heat causes it to melt and liquefy,
And either of these is a cause of fear for the bees.
It's for this reason they vie with one another
To smear wax over the chinks in the walls of their houses,
Or stop them up with resinous stuff from flowers,
More sticky than birdlime or pitch of Phrygian Ida—
They bring it home and save it for this purpose.
And, so we're told, sometimes they establish their house
In a hiding place underground, to keep themselves safe,
Or they're discovered to have settled themselves
In the cells within a porous rock, or maybe
The cavity of a tree's decaying trunk.
So help them out, by spreading mud or clay
Over the walls of their hive, and maybe scatter
A few leaves over it, too. Be sure there isn't

neu propius tectis taxum sine, neve rubentis
ure foco cancros, altae neu crede paludi,
aut ubi odor caeni gravis aut ubi concava pulsu
saxa sonant vocisque offensa resultat imago.

Quod superest, ubi pulsam hiemem Sol aureus egit
sub terras caelumque aestiva luce reclusit,
illae continuo saltus silvasque peragrant
purpureosque metunt flores et flumina libant
summa leves. hinc nescio qua dulcedine laetae
progeniem nidosque fovent, hinc arte recentis
excudunt ceras et mella tenacia fingunt.
hinc ubi iam emissum caveis ad sidera caeli
nare per aestatem liquidam suspexeris agmen
obscuramque trahi vento mirabere nubem,
contemplator: aquas dulcis et frondea semper
tecta petunt. huc tu iussos adsperge sapores,
trita melisphylla et cerinthae ignobile gramen,
tinnitusque cie et Matris quate cymbala circum.
ipsae consident medicatis sedibus, ipsae
intima more suo sese in cunabula condent.

Sin autem ad pugnam exierint—nam saepe duobus
regibus incessit magno discordia motu;
continuoque animos vulgi et trepidantia bello

A yew tree growing too near where the hive is placed;
Beware of roasting crab too close to it, too—
The smoke is poisonous to the bees; beware
Of any place where the smell of mud prevails,
Or where a voice from within a hollow rock
Comes echoing back in response to the sound that struck it.

When the golden sun has driven winter back down
Under the earth and opened up the sky
With the radiance of summer, then the bees
Fly everywhere through all the groves and glades,
Gathering from the beautiful flowers and lightly
Imbibing from the surface of the streams.
It's thus that, motivated by some joy
I know not how to name, they go about
The caring for their offspring and their nests;
It's thus that artfully they make new wax
And shape and form and mold their clinging honey.
And so, when you look up and see the swarm,
Emancipated from the hive and floating
Up to the starry sky through the summer air,
Or when you wonder at the sight of a dark
Cloud carried along and drifting on the wind,
Take heed, for there they are, on the hunt for leafy
Shelter near sweet water. There you should scatter
Scents as I prescribe—melísphyllum
And the common healing herb that's known as beebread;
And let there be the sound of tinkling bells
And the cymbals of Cybele, the Mighty Mother.
The bees will settle, of themselves, upon
The scented settling places you've prepared,
And of themselves will hide themselves within
The inner recesses of their cradling home.

But if they come out to do battle—for warfare often
With great disturbance breaks out between two kings—
You can sense their rage and excitement getting ready,

corda licet longe praesciscere; namque morantis
Martius ille aeris rauci canor increpat et vox
auditur fractos sonitus imitata tubarum;
tum trepidae inter se coeunt pinnisque coruscant
spiculaque exacuunt rostris aptantque lacertos
et circa regem atque ipsa ad praetoria densae
miscentur magnisque vocant clamoribus hostem:
ergo ubi ver nactae sudum camposque patentis,
erumpunt portis: concurritur, aethere in alto
fit sonitus, magnum mixtae glomerantur in orbem
praecipitesque cadunt; non densior aëre grando,
nec de concussa tantum pluit ilice glandis.
ipsi per medias acies insignibus alis
ingentis animos angusto in pectore versant,
usque adeo obnixi non cedere, dum gravis aut hos
aut hos versa fuga victor dare terga subegit.
hi motus animorum atque haec certamina tanta
pulveris exigui iactu compressa quiescent.

    Verum ubi ductores acie revocaveris ambo,
deterior qui visus, eum, ne prodigus obsit,
dede neci; melior vacua sine regnet in aula.
alter erit maculis auro squalentibus ardens
nam duo sunt genera: hic melior, insignis et ore
et rutilis clarus squamis; ille horridus alter
desidia latamque trahens inglorius alvum.
ut binae regum facies, ita corpora plebis.
namque aliae turpes horrent, ceu pulvere ab alto
cum venit et sicco terram spuit ore viator
aridus; elucent aliae et fulgore coruscant
ardentes auro et paribus lita corpora guttis.

As the hoarse pulsing warfare music sounds,
Like raucous trumpets summoning to the fight;
Then agitated they all crowd in together,
With quivering wings, getting their weapons ready,
Busily using their beaks to sharpen their stings,
Then swarm around the king and the royal tent
And with a great din challenge the enemy army.
It's thus that in the spring, when the day is clear
And the field is bright, they burst forth from their gates
And the battle's joined, the noise of it is heard
In the upper air, the hostile armies embroiled
In a great pulsating globe of clashing bees
That then precipitately falls to the ground,
Thicker than hail that rains down from the sky
Or acorns falling from a shaken oak.
In the thick of it, arrayed with splendid wings,
The kings themselves, great hearts in tiny bodies,
Fight on and lead the fight, refusing to yield,
Persisting till the final moment when
The one or the other one, victorious,
Will drive the vanquished to turn their backs and flee.
A little dust thrown down upon the scene
Will quiet this contention and this fury.

But once you've gotten both kings back from the battle,
Ascertain which is inferior in body,
And kill him so he won't be a waste of your time,
And let the better one reign alone in his palace.
There are two kinds of kings, one of them blazoned
With orange and ruddy-golden glittering scales;
The other one's disheveled, lazy-looking,
Ignobly trailing a fat belly behind him;
And if the kings are different from each other,
So is it with the commoners' bodies too:
Some of them are offensive to the sight,
As when, covered with dust, a wayfarer comes
Up from the wasteland desert spitting out dirt
From his dry parched mouth; the others' bodies shine
With light flashing from flecks and spots of gold.

haec potior suboles, hinc caeli tempore certo
dulcia mella premes, nec tantum dulcia, quantum
et liquida et durum Bacchi domitura saporem.
    At cum incerta volant caeloque examina ludunt
contemnuntque favos et frigida tecta relinquunt,
instabilis animos ludo prohibebis inani.
nec magnus prohibere labor: tu regibus alas
eripe; non illis quisquam cunctantibus altum
ire iter aut castris audebit vellere signa.
invitent croceis halantes floribus horti
et custos furum atque avium cum falce saligna
Hellespontiaci servet tutela Priapi.
ipse thymum tinosque ferens de montibus altis
tecta serat late circum, cui talia curae;
ipse labore manum duro terat, ipse feracis
figat humo plantas et amicos inriget imbres.
    Atque equidem, extremo ni iam sub fine laborum
vela traham et terris festinem advertere proram,
forsitan et, pinguis hortos quae cura colendi
ornaret, canerem, biferique rosaria Paesti,
quoque modo potis gauderent intiba rivis
et virides apio ripae, tortusque per herbam
cresceret in ventrem cucumis; nec sera comantem
narcissum aut flexi tacuissem vimen acanthi

These are the better kind; from them you'll have
Honey that's sweet yet not only sweet but clear,
Just right for subduing wine that tastes too strong.

But when the bees are heedless of their combs
And, letting the hives grow cold, are flying about,
Just playing around in the sunshine, you have to learn
To prohibit their feckless hearts from such aimless frolic.
It's easy enough to do: tear off the wings
Of the monarch bee; when he's unable to fly
The rest of them won't dare to leave their camp.
And you should make it attractive for them to stay
By planting gardens of sweet-smelling saffron flowers,
And let the guardian god Priápus be
Stationed there with his willow instrument
To guard them against both thieves and birds, and let
The man whose charge it is to care for them
Bring garden pines and thyme down from the hills
And set them out around their dwelling places
And encourage the plantings with friendly irrigation.

And, to be sure, if it were not true that I
Have nearly come to the end of this my labor
And now am almost ready to turn my vessel
Eagerly toward home and furl my sails,
It might be that I'd sing to celebrate
The care it takes to cultivate the flowers
That make our gardens beautiful. I'd sing
Of Paestum and its roses and how they bloom
Twice every year, and how the endive drinks
With gladness from the brooks, and how the green
Wild-celery plants adorn the riverbanks,
And the cucumber tendril winds and turns and coils
Its way through the grass, and swells and becomes its fruit.
Nor would I refrain from singing of narcissus,
Which blooms so late in the year, pale ivy, or

pallentisque hederas et amantis litora myrtos.
namque sub Oebaliae memini me turribus arcis,
qua niger umectat flaventia culta Galaesus,
Corycium vidisse senem, cui pauca relicti
iugera ruris erant, nec fertilis illa iuvencis
nec pecori opportuna seges nec commoda Baccho:
hic rarum tamen in dumis olus albaque circum
lilia verbenasque premens vescumque papaver
regum aequabat opes animis, seraque revertens
nocte domum dapibus mensas onerabat inemptis.
primus vere rosam atque autumno carpere poma,
et cum tristis hiems etiamnum frigore saxa
rumperet et glacie cursus frenaret aquarum,
ille comam mollis iam tondebat hyacinthi
aestatem increpitans seram Zephyrosque morantis.
ergo apibus fetis idem atque examine multo
primus abundare et spumantia cogere pressis
mella favis; illi tiliae atque uberrima tinus,
quotque in flore novo pomis se fertilis arbos
induerat, totidem autumno matura tenebat.
ille etiam seras in versum distulit ulmos
eduramque pirum et spinos iam pruna ferentis
iamque ministrantem platanum potantibus umbras.
verum haec ipse equidem spatiis exclusus iniquis
praetereo atque aliis post me memoranda relinquo.

The trailing stems of acanthus, or the myrtle
That loves to grow on banks beside the sea.
For I remember, down by Tárentum,
Where dark Galaesus waters the yellowing grain,
I saw an old Corýcian man, who lived there,
Under the arches and towers of the fort,
On a little patch of land that nobody wanted,
Too poor for oxen to plow, unfit for pasture,
Not right for planting vines. But this old man
Carefully planted white lilies, vervain, and poppies,
And different sorts of vegetables for his table,
And thus he made for himself a happiness
That was equal to the happiness of kings,
And when he came home at night his feast was free.
He was the first in spring to gather roses
And the first to gather apples in the fall,
And even while gloomy winter still persisted,
Splitting the rocks with freezing cold and holding
Rivers back in their courses with choking ice,
The old man was already out there, getting ready,
Cutting back last year's soft-haired hyacinth growth,
And scolding summer and its summer breezes
For being so late about returning again.
And so it was that he was always the first
To have multitudes of bees and therefore the first
To press the foaming honey from the comb;
The pine trees and the limes he planted flourished,
And the other fruit trees, too, lavish in blossom,
And, ripening into autumn, lavish in yield;
He planted rows of elms already matured,
And hardy pear trees already bearing fruit,
Blackthorns hung with their engrafted plums,
And planes, though young, yet old enough to provide
Shade for drinking wine beneath their boughs.
But I, compelled by the limits of my song,
Must leave his story for later chroniclers.

Nunc age, naturas apibus quas Iuppiter ipse
addidit expediam, pro qua mercede canoros
Curetum sonitus crepitantiaque aera secutae
Dictaeo caeli regem pavere sub antro.
solae communis natos, consortia tecta
urbis habent, magnisque agitant sub legibus aevum.
et patriam solae et certos novere penates,
venturaeque hiemis memores aestate laborem
experiuntur et in medium quaesita reponunt.
namque aliae victu invigilant et foedere pacto
exercentur agris; pars intra saepta domorum
narcissi lacrimam et lentum de cortice gluten
prima favis ponunt fundamina, deinde tenacis
suspendunt ceras; aliae spem gentis adultos
educunt fetus; aliae purissima mella
stipant et liquido distendunt nectare cellas;
sunt quibus ad portas cecidit custodia sorti,
inque vicem speculantur aquas et nubila caeli,
aut onera accipiunt venientum, aut agmine facto
ignavum fucos pecus a praesepibus arcent:
fervet opus, redolentque thymo fragrantia mella.
ac veluti lentis Cyclopes fulmina massis
cum properant, alii taurinis follibus auras
accipiunt redduntque, alii stridentia tingunt
aera lacu; gemit impositis incudibus Aetna;

Now therefore it is time to give an account
Of the nature of the bees and the way they live,
Ordained for them by Jupiter himself,
Rewarding them for the day they heard the music
And the clanging of the cymbals of the Curétes
And followed to the Cave of Dicte where
They fed the king of heaven hidden there.

They are the only ones who share their children
In common parentage, the only ones
To share in common the houses where they dwell;
They live together under the rule of law.
It is only they who have a common country
And share an unchanging home, and in the summer,
Knowing that winter is coming, their enterprise
Is to gather together what they'll have in common.
For some the charge and obligation is
To labor in the fields; for others, the task
Is to begin to build the honeycomb,
Spreading the resinous tears of the narcissus
And gluey stuff brought in from the bark of trees,
And building partition walls of clinging wax;
Others are charged with bringing up the young,
The nation's hope, to enter into adulthood;
Others pack purest honey into the cells
That swell and enlarge, infused with liquid nectar;
The task of others is to guard the doors
And watch the skies for signs of clouds and rain,
And accept into the hive the bees returning,
Carrying what they're bringing from the fields,
And, as an armed patrol, to drive away
The lazy crowd of drones from the busy stalls.

The community is glowing as it works;
The honey is fragrant with the scent of thyme.
They're like the Cyclops as they busily forge
Their weapons from the heavy ore of the mine,
Some of them working the pumping oxhide bellows,
And others plunging the iron rods they'd made

illi inter sese magna vi bracchia tollunt
in numerum, versantque tenaci forcipe ferrum:
non aliter, si parva licet componere magnis,
Cecropias innatus apes amor urget habendi
munere quamque suo. grandaevis oppida curae
et munire favos et daedala fingere tecta.
at fessae multa referunt se nocte minores,
crura thymo plenae; pascuntur et arbuta passim
et glaucas salices casiamque crocumque rubentem
et pinguem tiliam et ferrugineos hyacinthos.
omnibus una quies operum, labor omnibus unus:
mane ruunt portis, nusquam mora; rursus easdem
Vesper ubi e pastu tandem decedere campis
admonuit, tum tecta petunt, tum corpora curant;
fit sonitus, mussantque oras et limina circum.
post, ubi iam thalamis se composuere, siletur
in noctem, fessosque sopor suus occupat artus.
nec vero a stabulis pluvia impendente recedunt
longius, aut credunt caelo adventantibus Euris,
sed circum tutae sub moenibus urbis aquantur
excursusque brevis temptant, et saepe lapillos,
ut cumbae instabiles fluctu iactante saburram,

Into the hissing lake, and Aetna groaning
Under the anvils as they pound them, and
All the giants together one after the other
In rhythmic order raising their arms with mighty
Power to strike again in rhythmic order,
And all together turning the iron with tongs.
If little things can be compared to great,
Innate desire to work for the common wealth
Inspires the bees, and each of them has his role.
The care of the older bees is for the town,
The construction of the hives, the artful making
Of the houses where they dwell; the younger bees,
Late in the night, come wearily flying home,
Their legs weighed down with thyme they've pastured on,
Arbutus, gray willow, marjoram, ruby crocus,
Rich linden blossoms, and dusky hyacinth.
One time for all to rest, one time to labor.
Thus, early in the morning out they rush,
Pouring forth from their gates; not one holds back;
And then, when early evening comes around
And Vesper tells them it's time for them to leave
Their foraging in the fields, back home they come,
And you can hear their murmuring humming as
They groom themselves and hither and thither flit
Around the doors and thresholds of their houses;
And after that, when they compose themselves
To rest within their chambers, and sound sleep
Possesses their bodies weary from their labors,
All through the night the bees are utterly silent.

On days when rain is coming they don't go far
Away from their hives, nor do they fly high up
When East Wind gales are blowing; they stay in near
The safe walls of their town, looking for water,
And flying low. And sometimes in their flights,
As wallowing vessels often carry ballast
To steady themselves in choppy waters, the bees
Will carry little pebbles to balance themselves
And keep them steady in the unstable air.

tollunt, his sese per inania nubila librant.
saepe etiam duris errando in cotibus alas
attrivere, ultroque animam sub fasce dedere:
tantus amor florum et generandi gloria mellis.

Illum adeo placuisse apibus mirabere morem,
quod neque concubitu indulgent, nec corpora segnes
in Venerem solvunt aut fetus nixibus edunt;
verum ipsae e foliis natos, e suavibus herbis
ore legunt, ipsae regem parvosque Quirites
sufficiunt, aulasque et cerea regna refingunt.
ergo ipsas quamvis angusti terminus aevi
excipiat (neque enim plus septima ducitur aestas),
at genus immortale manet, multosque per annos
stat fortuna domus, et avi numerantur avorum.

Praeterea regem non sic Aegyptus et ingens
Lydia nec populi Parthorum aut Medus Hydaspes
observant. rege incolumi mens omnibus una est;
amisso rupere fidem, constructaque mella
diripuere ipsae et crates solvere favorum.
ille operum custos, illum admirantur et omnes
circumstant fremitu denso stipantque frequentes,
et saepe attollunt umeris et corpora bello
obiectant pulchramque petunt per vulnera mortem.

It happens often that as, heavily laden,
They wander among hard rocks, their wings are bruised
And so they lose their lives—such is their love
For flowers and the glory of making honey.

❦

And you will be surprised that the bees are never
Known to indulge in sexual intercourse; they never
Dissipate or enervate their bodies
By making love; they do not bring forth children
By labor of birth; instead, they gather them
By plucking the little babies with their mouths
From the leaves of trees and from the sweetest herbs.
This is the way they produce a succeeding monarch
And all the new little citizens of the realm,
And they themselves refashion and renew
Their palaces and waxen halls; and so,
Though only a narrow period of time
Defines how long the life of each will last
(It's never longer than past the seventh summer),
The race persists in immortality,
Its fortunes maintained for many generations,
Grandsire down from grandsire down from grandsire.

Neither Egypt nor great Lydia nor the tribes
Of Parthia nor the Hydaspéian Medes
Pay homage such as these to their royal master:
As long as he is safe, they are united;
He being lost, the bond of their allegiance
Is broken, and they pull to pieces the honey
That they themselves constructed, and tear apart
The articulated honeycombs they made.
The chieftain is the guardian of their labor;
They worship him and follow him and make
A great clamoring noise as they crowd around him;
Often they lift him up upon their shoulders
And carry him about to show their fealty;

His quidam signis atque haec exempla secuti
esse apibus partem divinae mentis et haustus
aetherios dixere; deum namque ire per omnia,
terrasque tractusque maris caelumque profundum;
hinc pecudes, armenta, viros, genus omne ferarum,
quemque sibi tenuis nascentem arcessere vitas;
scilicet huc reddi deinde ac resoluta referri
omnia, nec morti esse locum, sed viva volare
sideris in numerum atque alto succedere caelo.
    Si quando sedem angustam servataque mella
thesauris relines, prius haustu sparsus aquarum
ora fove, fumosque manu praetende sequacis.
illis ira modum supra est, laesaeque venenum
morsibus inspirant, et spicula caeca relinquunt
adfixae venis, animasque in vulnere ponunt.
bis gravidos cogunt fetus, duo tempora messis,
Taygete simul os terris ostendit honestum
Plias et Oceani spretos pede reppulit amnis,
aut eadem sidus fugiens ubi Piscis aquosi
tristior hibernas caelo descendit in undas.
sin duram metues hiemem parcesque futuro
contususosque animos et res miserabere fractas,

They put their bodies in danger for him in wars
And seek a noble death amid the carnage.

Because of such signs and instances, some say
The bees have drunk from the light of heaven and have
A share in the divine intelligence,
For the god, they say, is there in everything
In earth and the range of sea and the depth of sky;
The flocks, the herds, and men, all creatures there are,
At birth derive their little lives from him,
And when they die their life returns to him,
And having been unmade is made again;
There is, they say, no place at all for death;
The life of beings flies up to the stars
And finds its place there in the heaven above.

Whenever you think it's time to open up
Their narrow houses to get at the honey treasure
They've hoarded there, first you must freshen your mouth
With a little water, and hold out a smoking stick
In front of you in your hand as you reach in:
Do this to sedate the bees and keep them calm.
The raging of the bees when they're disturbed
Is more than violent; their bite's suffused
With poison, and they leave their stingers fixed
In the veins they attack, and give up their lives to do it.

Two times a year the rich produce is gathered;
Two harvests a year; the first of them takes place
When the Pleiad Táygeté with disdainful foot
Is taking her leave of the waters of the sea
To show her beautiful face to the waiting earth;
The other is when the very same star, in flight
From rainy Pisces, sadly descends from the sky
To disappear beneath the wintry waves.

But if you have reason to fear there's going to be
A hard winter ahead, and you want to protect

at suffire thymo cerasque recidere inanis
quis dubitet? nam saepe favos ignotus adedit
stellio et lucifugis congesta cubilia blattis
immunisque sedens aliena ad pabula fucus;
aut asper crabro imparibus se immiscuit armis,
aut dirum tiniae genus, aut invisa Minervae
laxos in foribus suspendit aranea cassis.
quo magis exhaustae fuerint, hoc acrius omnes
incumbent generis lapsi sarcire ruinas
complebuntque foros et floribus horrea texent.

    Si vero, quoniam casus apibus quoque nostros
vita tulit, tristi languebunt corpora morbo—
quod iam non dubiis poteris cognoscere signis:
continuo est aegris alius color; horrida vultum
deformat macies; tum corpora luce carentum
exportant tectis et tristia funera ducunt;
aut illae pedibus conexae ad limina pendent,
aut intus clausis cunctantur in aedibus omnes
ignavaeque fame et contracto frigore pigrae.
tum sonus auditur gravior, tractimque susurrant,
frigidus ut quondam silvis immurmurat Auster,
ut mare sollicitum stridit refluentibus undis,
aestuat ut clausis rapidus fornacibus ignis.

The bees against the future, guarding against
The shattering of their hopes and of their spirits,
Why would you hesitate to help them out
By fumigating the hive with the smoke of thyme
And clearing out the empty waxen cells?
Sometimes a newt has secretly gotten at
The honeycomb and nibbled it, sometimes
The beetles that hide from the light have gotten into
The congested chambers of the hive, or else
The drone, freeloader, feasts from another's table,
Fierce wasps come in with overwhelming forces,
The moth, the creature of a dreaded race,
Or the spider that Minerva hates, that hangs
Loose curtains in the doorways of their houses.
The greater the devastation the more the bees
Urgently work together to restore
The ruins of their fallen nations, refilling
Their rows of honeycomb cells, refurbishing
Their storage rooms with gum brought back from flowers.

It's true for bees as it is for human beings:
Life brings sickness with it. You can see
The signs of it in the bees, without any doubt:
Their color changes as soon as they fall ill;
Their bodies are all disheveled and there's a dreadful
Emaciation in the look of them;
And then you can see the other bees as they carry
Out from the dwelling places the bodies of those
From whom the life has gone; and you can see
The sick ones not yet dead that hang almost
Motionless around the doors outside,
With crossed and tangled feet; or still inside,
Listless with hunger and shrunken from the cold.
And then you can hear a mournful long-drawn-out
Whispering rustling sound like the sound of the cold
South Wind as it murmurs in the woods, or like
The agitated hissing of the sea

hic iam galbaneos suadebo incendere odores
mellaque harundineis inferre canalibus, ultro
hortantem et fessas ad pabula nota vocantem.
proderit et tunsum gallae admiscere saporem
arentisque rosas, aut igni pinguia multo
defruta vel psithia passos de vite racemos,
Cecropiumque thymum et grave olentia centaurea.
est etiam flos in pratis, cui nomen amello
fecere agricolae, facilis quaerentibus herba;
namque uno ingentem tollit de caespite silvam,
aureus ipse, sed in foliis, quae plurima circum
funduntur, violae sublucet purpura nigrae;
saepe deum nexis ornatae torquibus arae;
asper in ore sapor; tonsis in vallibus illum
pastores et curva legunt prope flumina Mellae.
huius odorato radices incoque Baccho
pabulaque in foribus plenis appone canistris.
        Sed si quem proles subito defecerit omnis
nec genus unde novae stirpis revocetur habebit,
tempus et Arcadii memoranda inventa magistri
pandere, quoque modo caesis iam saepe iuvencis
insincerus apes tulerit cruor. altius omnem
expediam prima repetens ab origine famam.
nam qua Pellaei gens fortunata Canopi
accolit effuso stagnantem flumine Nilum
et circum pictis vehitur sua rura phaselis,
quaque pharetratae vicinia Persidis urget,
et diversa ruens septem discurrit in ora
usque coloratis amnis devexus ab Indis,
et viridem Aegyptum nigra fecundat harena,
omnis in hac certam regio iacit arte salutem.

As the waves draw back, or the seething noise of a fire
Eating its way as it burns inside a furnace.
At such a time you must offer them the odor
Of the smoke of sweet-smelling resin, and feed them honey
Through oaten straws, to encourage the weary creatures
And invite them to partake of accustomed food;
A good idea, as well, to offer dried
Rose leaves in a mixture with powdered oak-gall,
Or must that has been enriched by boiling down,
Or sun-dried clusters of Psithian grapes, together
With aromatic centaurium and thyme;
And there's a meadow plant that's called "amellus,"
Easy to see because from a single root
One stem produces an enormous fountain
Of golden cascading leaves and among them shining
Dark-purple-violet lights of the flower petals;
These often garland the altars of the gods.
It has a bitter taste; it's gathered by
The shepherds where they find them in the pastures
Or on the banks of wandering Mella's stream.
You should boil the roots in fragrant wine and leave
The food set out in baskets near their doors.

But if it suddenly happens that the whole
Stock is utterly lost and you don't know how
To go about establishing another,
It's time to disclose the legendary secrets
Of the Arcadian master, by means of which
Bees were engendered from the putrid blood
Of a slaughtered bullock. I will go back to the very
Origin of the legend to tell about it,
For where the fortunate Canópians live,
By the quivered Parthians' borders, in the delta
Of the seven mouths of the river Nile that flows
Downhill from the swarthy Indians' country and makes
Egypt so fecund with alluvial soil,
And where they sail their painted skiffs on fields
Where the river waters flooded and grew still,
Their safety depends on their knowledge of this art.

Exiguus primum atque ipsos contractus in usus
eligitur locus; hunc angustique imbrice tecti
parietibusque premunt artis, et quattuor addunt
quattuor a ventis obliqua luce fenestras.
tum vitulus bima curvans iam cornua fronte
quaeritur; huic geminae nares et spiritus oris
multa reluctanti obstruitur, plagisque perempto
tunsa per integram solvuntur viscera pellem.
sic positum in clauso linquunt et ramea costis
subiciunt fragmenta, thymum casiasque recentis.
hoc geritur Zephyris primum impellentibus undas,
ante novis rubeant quam prata coloribus, ante
garrula quam tignis nidum suspendat hirundo.
interea teneris tepefactus in ossibus umor
aestuat, et visenda modis animalia miris,
trunca pedum primo, mox et stridentia pinnis,
miscentur, tenuemque magis magis aëra carpunt,
donec ut aestivis effusus nubibus imber
erupere, aut ut nervo pulsante sagittae,
prima leves ineunt si quando proelia Parthi.
    Quis deus hanc, Musae, quis nobis extudit artem?
unde nova ingressus hominum experientia cepit?
pastor Aristaeus fugiens Peneia Tempe,
amissis, ut fama, apibus morboque fameque,
tristis ad extremi sacrum caput astitit amnis,

First, choose for this purpose a very constricted place,
In which, to constrict it further, then construct
A narrow shed, roofed with a roof of tile,
And close it in with walls close in together,
And in the four walls toward the four winds set
Four windows letting in the light aslant;
And then select a bullock two summers old,
His new first horns emerging on his brow,
And get the bullock into the shed, and then,
Although he struggles against it, stuff up his nostrils
And stop up the breath in his mouth, and after that,
Beat him to death until his innards collapse
Inside his hide; and as his body lies there
Put broken branches around him in the shed,
And marjoram and thyme, and leave him there.
This should be done when the zephyrs with their touch
Have just begun to quicken and stir the waves
And just before the meadows begin to blush
With their new color and just before the chattering
Swallow hangs her nest from the high house-rafters.
Meanwhile the fluid grows warm in his softening bones,
And it ferments, and wonderful new creatures
Come into view, footless at first, but soon
With humming wings; they swarm, and more and more
Try out their wings on the empty air, and then
Burst forth like a summer shower from summer clouds
Or like a shower of arrows from the bows
Of Parthian warriors entering the fray.
What god was it, O Muses, who devised
An art like this? Where was it that such strange
New knowledge came from and was learned by men?

As the story is told, the shepherd Aristáeus,
As by Penéus he prepared to leave
The vale of Tempe, after it had happened
That because of sickness or starvation all
His stock of bees was lost, lamenting stood

multa querens, atque hac adfatus voce parentem:
"mater, Cyrene mater, quae gurgitis huius
ima tenes, quid me praeclara stirpe deorum
(si modo, quem perhibes, pater est Thymbraeus Apollo)
invisum fatis genuisti? aut quo tibi nostri
pulsus amor? quid me caelum sperare iubebas?
en etiam hunc ipsum vitae mortalis honorem,
quem mihi vix frugum et pecudum custodia sollers
omnia temptanti extuderat, te matre relinquo.
quin age et ipsa manu felicis erue silvas,
fer stabulis inimicum ignem atque interfice messes,
ure sata et validam in vitis molire bipennem,
tanta meae si te ceperunt taedia laudis."
  At mater sonitum thalamo sub fluminis alti
sensit. eam circum Milesia vellera Nymphae
carpebant, hyali saturo fucata colore,
Drymoque Xanthoque Ligeaque Phyllodoceque,
caesariem effusae nitidam per candida colla,
Nesaee Spioque Thaliaque Cymodoceque,
Cydippe et flava Lycorias, altera virgo,
altera tum primos Lucinae experta labores,
Clioque et Beroe soror, Oceanitides ambae,
ambae auro, pictis incinctae pellibus ambae,
atque Ephyre atque Opis et Asia Deiopea
et tandem positis velox Arethusa sagittis.
inter quas curam Clymene narrabat inanem
Volcani Martisque dolos et dulcia furta,
aque Chao densos divum numerabat amores.

By the sacred source from which the river arose,
And cried out to his mother this complaint:

"O Mother, Cyréné, Mother, you who live
Here in this whirlpool, why did you give birth
To me in the glorious lineage of the gods—
If it is true that, as you say, my father
Was Thýmbraean Apollo—that I should be
So hated by the Fates? Or what has caused you
So to reject the love you had for me?
Why did you foster in me the hope of heaven?
Now even the honor that by hard-wrought skill
I have achieved through all my mortal effort,
To bring the crops in safely against all odds,
And to care for all the creatures of the farm,
Mother, I here renounce. If you are seized
By hatred for the work that I have done,
Cut down my fruitful woods, burn down my barns,
Destroy my crops and the seeds that make new crops,
And take an ax and slash my vines to the ground."

His mother heard the cry in her chamber, deep
In the waters of the river; the Nymphs around her
Were spinning wool of Milétus that was dyed
In many translucent hues and tincts, their shining
Long hair flowing about their snow-white necks,
Drymo, and Xantho, Ligea, Phyllodócé,
Cýdippé, and golden-haired Lycórias,
(The one a virgin maiden, the other having
Just begun to experience the first
Signs of the labors that Lucína fosters),
And the daughters of Ocean, Clio and Beróe,
Both of them clad in dappled deerskin garments
And both arrayed in ornaments of gold,
Ephyré, Opis and Asian Déiopéa,
Swift Arethúsa, her arrows put aside.
And in the midst was Clýmené, telling stories,
Stories of lovelorn Vulcan, and of Mars's
Stratagems and furtive stolen pleasures,

carmine quo captae dum fusis mollia pensa
devolvunt, iterum maternas impulit auris
luctus Aristaei, vitreisque sedilibus omnes
obstipuere; sed ante alias Arethusa sorores
prospiciens summa flavum caput extulit unda,
et procul: "o gemitu non frustra exterrita tanto,
Cyrene soror, ipse tibi, tua maxima cura,
tristis Aristaeus nostri genitoris ad undam
stat lacrimans, et te crudelem nomine dicit."
    Huic percussa nova mentem formidine mater
"duc, age, duc ad nos; fas illi limina divum
tangere" ait: simul alta iubet discedere late
flumina, qua iuvenis gressus inferret. at illum
curvata in montis faciem circumstetit unda,
accepitque sinu vasto misitque sub amnem.
iamque domum mirans genetricis et umida regna
speluncisque lacus clausos lucosque sonantis
ibat, et ingenti motu stupefactus aquarum
omnia sub magna labentia flumina terra
spectabat diversa locis, Phasimque Lycumque
et caput, unde altus primum se erumpit Enipeus,
unde pater Tiberinus et unde Aniena fluenta
saxosusque sonans Hypanis Mysusque Caicus,
et gemina auratus taurino cornua vultu
Eridanus, quo non alius per pinguia culta

And telling all the numerous loves of gods
Since Chaos the beginning of the world.

And as the company of Nymphs attended
To the stories she was telling, captivated,
The soft wool purling from their turning spindles,
Suddenly Aristáeus's loud lament
Was heard by his mother's ears a second time,
And all the Nymphs, on their crystal thrones, were startled.
But Arethúsa went up to the water's surface
And raised her golden head above the waves
And looked, and called back down from far above,
And said: "Cyréné, Sister, not without reason
Have you been struck with fear because you heard
This loud lamenting cry. It is your son.
Your most dear Aristáeus weeping stands
On the riverbank of the waters of our father,
Accusing you, by name, of cruelty."

The mother, struck with dread, replied to her:
"O bring him here, bring him to me; he is
Permitted to cross the threshold of the gods."
And saying this she caused the mighty streams
To draw apart, so that the youth could enter;
The streams like mountains stood arched high around him,
Admitting him down into the vast recess,
And welcoming him therein. And so he entered,
Amazed at his mother's house, the realm of waters,
Amazed at the lakes locked in the caverns down there,
And the groves of echoing rock, and stupefied
By the mighty noise of all the rivers there are,
Each of them flowing its way in its own direction,
The Phasis, and the Lycus, and the source
From which Enípeus rises and breaks forth,
And Father Tiber, and Hýpanis roaring down
Along its bouldered course, and Mýsian
Caïcus and the Po, the bellowing bull
Whose charging forehead has two golden horns—
No river has more violent force than this

in mare purpureum violentior effluit amnis.
postquam est in thalami pendentia pumice tecta
perventum et nati fletus cognovit inanis
Cyrene, manibus liquidos dant ordine fontis
germanae, tonsisque ferunt mantelia villis;
pars epulis onerant mensas et plena reponunt
pocula, Panchaeis adolescunt ignibus arae.
et mater "cape Maeonii carchesia Bacchi:
Oceano libemus" ait: simul ipsa precatur
Oceanumque patrem rerum Nymphasque sorores,
centum quae silvas, centum quae flumina servant.
ter liquido ardentem perfundit nectare Vestam,
ter flamma ad summum tecti subiecta reluxit.
omine quo firmans animum sic incipit ipsa:
    "Est in Carpathio Neptuni gurgite vates,
caeruleus Proteus, magnum qui piscibus aequor
et iuncto bipedum curru metitur equorum.
hic nunc Emathiae portus patriamque revisit
Pallenen; hunc et Nymphae veneramur et ipse
grandaevus Nereus; novit namque omnia vates,
quae sint, quae fuerint, quae mox ventura trahantur;
quippe ita Neptuno visum est, immania cuius
armenta et turpis pascit sub gurgite phocas.
hic tibi, nate, prius vinclis capiendus, ut omnem
expediat morbi causam eventusque secundet.
nam sine vi non ulla dabit praecepta, neque illum
orando flectes; vim duram et vincula capto
tende; doli circum haec demum frangentur inanes.
ipsa ego te, medios cum sol accenderit aestus,

As through the cultivated fields it flows
And pours itself into the purple sea.

And when he had come into his mother's bower,
Beneath its pendent sheltering of stone,
And she had heard his sad lament, the sisters,
Each of them with her task, prepared the feast:
Pouring out pure spring water to wash his hands,
And offering smooth-shorn napkins; others set out
Delicacies for the feast, and drinking cups
And filled them full to the brim; the Panchaean-incense-
Perfumed fire blazed up upon the altars.
And then his mother said to Aristáeus:
"Take up the drinking cups of Maeónian wine
And let us pour a libation to Oceánus."
And she recited a prayer to Father Ocean
And to the sister Nymphs, the guardians
Of a hundred groves and of a hundred streams.
Three times the flame grew bright and rose to the roof.
When this encouraging omen had occurred,
These were the further words she spoke to her son:

"In Neptune's swirling Carpathian waters there's
A seer who measures the oceans in a car
Drawn by creatures half fish half two-footed horses.
This is the season when he returns to the ports
Of Thessaly and Palléne, his native home;
We Nymphs and old Néreus pay him homage
Because he, Proteus, knows all things there are:
What is; what once was; what will happen soon.
This is ordained by Neptune, for whom he shepherds
His herds of monsters and rank-smelling seals that pasture
Beneath the ocean waters. Seize him, my son,
And bind him fast in chains, so he will tell you
The causes of the disease and bring about
A fortunate outcome. But beware. He'll grant
No benefit of his wisdom, answer no prayers
Unless you force him to. So bind him tight,
The only way to render his trickery useless.

cum sitiunt herbae et pecori iam gratior umbra est,
in secreta senis ducam, quo fessus ab undis
se recipit, facile ut somno adgrediare iacentem.
verum ubi correptum manibus vinclisque tenebis,
tum variae eludent species atque ora ferarum.
fiet enim subito sus horridus atraque tigris
squamosusque draco et fulva cervice leaena,
aut acrem flammae sonitum dabit atque ita vinclis
excidet, aut in aquas tenuis dilapsus abibit.
sed quanto ille magis formas se vertet in omnis
tam tu, nate, magis contende tenacia vincla,
donec talis erit mutato corpore, qualem
videris, incepto tegeret cum lumina somno."
 Haec ait et liquidum ambrosiae defundit odorem,
quo totum nati corpus perduxit; at illi
dulcis compositis spiravit crinibus aura
atque habilis membris venit vigor. est specus ingens
exesi latere in montis, quo plurima vento
cogitur inque sinus scindit sese unda reductos,
deprensis olim statio tutissima nautis;
intus se vasti Proteus tegit obice saxi.
hic iuvenem in latebris aversum a lumine Nympha
collocat, ipsa procul nebulis obscura resistit.
iam rapidus torrens sitientis Sirius Indos
ardebat caelo, et medium sol igneus orbem
hauserat; arebant herbae, et cava flumina siccis

And I myself, in the heat of noon, and when
The pasture grass is thirsty and the herds
Are grateful to find the shady places to rest,
Will lead you to the old man's secret bower,
To which he retires when weary of the waves,
So you can seize him when he falls asleep.
But while you hold him with your hands and chains,
There will be images and forms and wild-beast shapes
That will bewilder you, for suddenly
There'll be a bristling wild boar there, there'll be
A fearsome tiger, a huge and scaly serpent,
A tawny-throated lioness, or else
He'll utter forth as a noise like roaring fire
And thus slip away from his bonds, or turn into water
And flow away that way. But keep the fetters tight,
Until he's gone through all the changes he has,
And comes back to being just what he was when you found him
Lying in his bower fast asleep."

She spoke, and the odor of purest ambrosia
Was everywhere; the fragrance of it breathed
In the hair of his head; his whole being received it,
Transforming him in bodily power and grace.

◄

There is an enormous grotto that the waves
The wind has driven in have hollowed out
In the high sea-cliffs that stand along the shore,
Sailors' safe haven sometimes when a storm
Has suddenly surprised them out at sea.
Within this cavern is where Proteus finds
Shelter behind a huge protecting rock.
Cyréné guided her son to where he was stationed
Out of the light and ready for the ambush,
And she herself stood, shrouded in mist, apart.
The torrid parching Dog Star blazed in the sky;
The fire of the sun had eaten up half its journey;
The meadow grasses were shriveled in the heat,

faucibus ad limum radii tepefacta coquebant,
cum Proteus consueta petens e fluctibus antra
ibat: eum vasti circum gens umida ponti
exsultans rorem late dispergit amarum.
sternunt se somno diversae in litore phocae;
ipse velut stabuli custos in montibus olim,
Vesper ubi e pastu vitulos ad tecta reducit
auditisque lupos acuunt balatibus agni,
considit scopulo medius, numerumque recenset.
cuius Aristaeo quoniam est oblata facultas,
vix defessa senem passus componere membra
cum clamore ruit magno, manicisque iacentem
occupat. ille suae contra non immemor artis
omnia transformat sese in miracula rerum,
ignemque horribilemque feram fluviumque liquentem.
verum ubi nulla fugam reperit fallacia, victus
in sese redit atque hominis tandem ore locutus
"nam quis te, iuvenum confidentissime, nostras
iussit adire domos? quidve hinc petis?" inquit. at ille
"scis, Proteu, scis ipse; neque est te fallere quicquam;
sed tu desine velle. deum praecepta secuti
venimus hinc lassis quaesitum oracula rebus."
tantum effatus. ad haec vates vi denique multa
ardentis oculos intorsit lumine glauco,
et graviter frendens sic fatis ora resolvit:

And the thirsting throats of the dry streambeds were baked
By the scorching rays right down to the hardened mud.
Proteus, seeking his usual cavern to rest in,
Came in from the sea. Around him as he came
A company of creatures of the deep
Leaped and cavorted and played among the waves,
Splashing the briny ocean spray around them.
Scattered in groups along the shore the seals
Were getting ready for sleep, and like a shepherd
Guarding his hillside flock when evening comes
And Vesper brings the young steers home from the pastures
And the bleating of the lambs excites the attention
Of listening wolves, Proteus seats himself
On a rock among his charges to count their number.

Then Aristáeus, as soon as he saw his chance,
Not giving him a moment, made a loud noise
And jumped out upon him and tied the old man up.
And Proteus, remembering his arts,
Changed himself into all kinds of wonderful things,
Fire, or frightful beast, or flowing water,
But when no trick of his would set him free,
Conquered he changed back into himself again,
And spoke with the voice of man: "Arrogant youth,
Who is it who has sent you to this my place?
What is it you're seeking? What is it that you want?"
"You, Proteus, know, you know because you know
All things that are; there's nothing that can deceive you;
Therefore it's time for you to give up your tricks.
The guidance of the gods has brought us here
To seek an oracle whose wisdom might
Give us the means to remedy our distress."
Then, overborne by force, at last the seer,
Grinding his teeth and rolling his sea-green eyes
To glare at Aristáeus, opened his mouth,
And uttered the words that told the fateful story:

◞

"Non te nullius exercent numinis irae;
magna luis commissa: tibi has miserabilis Orpheus
haudquaquam ad meritum poenas, ni fata resistant,
suscitat, et rapta graviter pro coniuge saevit.
illa quidem, dum te fugeret per flumina praeceps,
immanem ante pedes hydrum moritura puella
servantem ripas alta non vidit in herba.
at chorus aequalis Dryadum clamore supremos
implevit montis; flerunt Rhodopeiae arces
altaque Pangaea et Rhesi Mavortia tellus
atque Getae atque Hebrus et Actias Orithyia.
ipse cava solans aegrum testudine amorem
te, dulcis coniunx, te solo in litore secum,
te veniente die, te decedente canebat.
Taenarias etiam fauces, alta ostia Ditis,
et caligantem nigra formidine lucum
ingressus, Manisque adiit regemque tremendum
nesciaque humanis precibus mansuescere corda.
at cantu commotae Erebi de sedibus imis
umbrae ibant tenues simulacraque luce carentum,
quam multa in foliis avium se milia condunt,
Vesper ubi aut hibernus agit de montibus imber,
matres atque viri defunctaque corpora vita
magnanimum heroum, pueri innuptaeque puellae,
impositique rogis iuvenes ante ora parentum,
quos circum limus niger et deformis harundo

"It is a god, no less, who persecutes you;
The offense for which you're punished, though punished less
Than what you did deserves, is very great;
It's Orpheus, unless Fate intervenes,
Who rouses up these punishments against you,
And, inconsolable, rages over the loss
Of his dear wife Eurýdicé. She fled from you,
Headlong along the river, unhappy maiden,
And did not see the frightful snake that lurked
In the high grass, guarding the riverbank.
The cries of the sister band of dryads filled
The air as high as the mountaintops; the cliffs
Of Rhodope wept, the cliffs of Pangaea wept,
And the warrior land of the Getae, Oríthyia, Hebrus.
Alone upon the unfrequented shore
Orpheus, playing his lyre, sang to himself
His songs of you, dear wife, as day came on
With the light of the morning sun, and as the light
Descended in the evening. Singing he went
Down through the very throat of Táenarus,
The high gate of the dark kingdom of Dis,
And through the murky grove where Terror dwells
In black obscurity, and entered into
The Mané's place, the place of the dreadful King
And the hearts no human prayers can cause to pity.

And, set in motion by the sound of music,
From the lowest depths of Erebus there came,
As numerous as the many hundred birds
That, driven there by the coming on of evening
Or by a winter storm, fly in for shelter
In the foliage of a grove, the flittering shades,
The unsubstantial phantom shapes of those
For whom there is not any light at all—
Women and men, famous great-hearted heroes,
The life in their hero bodies now defunct,
Unmarried boys and girls, sons whom their fathers
Had had to watch being placed on the funeral pyre,
And all around them the hideous tangling reeds

Cocyti tardaque palus inamabilis unda
alligat et noviens Styx interfusa coercet.
quin ipsae stupuere domus atque intima Leti
Tartara caeruleosque implexae crinibus anguis
Eumenides, tenuitque inhians tria Cerberus ora,
atque Ixionii vento rota constitit orbis.
    "Iamque pedem referens casus evaserat omnis,
redditaque Eurydice superas veniebat ad auras,
pone sequens (namque hanc dederat Proserpina legem),
cum subita incautum dementia cepit amantem,
ignoscenda quidem, scirent si ignoscere Manes:
restitit, Eurydicenque suam iam luce sub ipsa
immemor heu! victusque animi respexit. ibi omnis
effusus labor atque immitis rupta tyranni
foedera, terque fragor stagnis auditus Averni.
illa 'quis et me' inquit 'miseram et te perdidit, Orpheu,
quis tantus furor? en iterum crudelia retro
fata vocant conditque natantia lumina somnus.
iamque vale: feror ingenti circumdata nocte
invalidasque tibi tendens, heu! non tua, palmas.'
dixit et ex oculis subito, ceu fumus in auras
commixtus tenuis, fugit diversa, neque illum
prensantem nequiquam umbras et multa volentem
dicere praeterea vidit; nec portitor Orci

And the black ooze of Cocýtos' swampy waters;
Nine times Styx wound its fettering chain around them.
And the house of Death was spellbound by his music,
All the way down to the bottom of Tártarus;
Spellbound the snakes in the hair of the Furies too;
And Cérberus the Hell-Dog's all three mouths
Were open-mouthed and silent, forgetting to bark;
The wind was still, and Ixíon's wheel stopped turning.

And now, as he was carefully going back
The way he came, and step by step avoiding
All possible wrong steps, and step by step
Eurýdicé, whom he was bringing back,
Unseen behind his back was following—
For this is what Proserpina had commanded—
They were coming very near the upper air,
And a sudden madness seized him, madness of love,
A madness to be forgiven if Hell but knew
How to forgive; he stopped in his tracks, and then,
Just as they were just about to emerge
Out into the light, suddenly, seized by love,
Bewildered into heedlessness, alas!
His purpose overcome, he turned, and looked
Back at Eurýdicé! And then and there
His labor was spilled and flowed away like water.
The implacable tyrant broke the pact: three times
The pools of Avérnus heard the sound of thunder.

'What was it,' she cried, 'what madness, Orpheus, was it,
That has destroyed us, you and me, oh look!
The cruel Fates already call me back,
And sleep is covering over my swimming eyes.
Farewell; I'm being carried off into
The vast surrounding dark and reaching out
My strengthless hands to you forever more
Alas not yours.' And saying this, like smoke
Disintegrating into air she was
Dispersed away and vanished from his eyes
And never saw him again, and he was left

amplius obiectam passus transire paludem.
quid faceret? quo se rapta bis coniuge ferret?
quo fletu manis, quae numina voce moveret?
illa quidem Stygia nabat iam frigida cumba.
septem illum totos perhibent ex ordine mensis
rupe sub aëria deserti ad Strymonis undam
flevisse, et gelidis haec evolvisse sub antris
mulcentem tigris et agentem carmine quercus:
qualis populea maerens philomela sub umbra
amissos queritur fetus, quos durus arator
observans nido implumis detraxit; at illa
flet noctem, ramoque sedens miserabile carmen
integrat, et maestis late loca questibus implet.
nulla Venus, non ulli animum flexere hymenaei:
solus Hyperboreas glacies Tanaimque nivalem
arvaque Riphaeis numquam viduata pruinis
lustrabat, raptam Eurydicen atque inrita Ditis
dona querens. spretae Ciconum quo munere matres
inter sacra deum nocturnique orgia Bacchi
discerptum latos iuvenem sparsere per agros.
tum quoque marmorea caput a cervice revulsum
gurgite cum medio portans Oeagrius Hebrus
volveret, Eurydicen vox ipsa et frigida lingua,
a miseram Eurydicen! anima fugiente vocabat:
Eurydicen toto referebant flumine ripae."

Clutching at shadows, with so much still to say.
And the boatman never again would take him across
The barrier of the marshy waters of Hell.
What could he do? His wife twice taken from him.
How could he bear it? How could his tears move Hell?
The Stygian boat has carried her away.

And, it is said that he, day after day,
For seven months beside the river Strymon,
Sat underneath a towering cliff, and wept,
And sang, and told in song his story; entranced,
The wild beasts listened; entranced, the oak trees moved
Closer to hear the song, which was like that
Of the nightingale, in the shade of a poplar tree,
In mourning for her children who were taken,
As yet unfledged, by a herdsman, hard of heart,
Who had happened upon the nest—she weeps all night
And over and over repeats her lamentation
And fills the listening air with her sad complaint.

No thought of marriage or any other love
Could turn his heart away from its bereavement.
Alone he roamed the Hyperborean North
And wandered along the snowy banks of the Don
Or through the barren frozen fields on the sides
Of Riphaean mountains, in grief for his lost wife
And Hades' empty promise, until the enraged
Cicónian Bacchantes, in a nocturnal
Ritual orgy, tore his body to pieces
And scattered the pieces everywhere, far and wide;
And as his head, cut off from his beautiful neck,
Was tumbling down the rushing course of Hebrus,
His voice and tongue, with his last breath, cried out,
'Eurýdicé! O poor Eurýdicé!'
And the banks of the downward river Hebrus echoed,
'O poor Eurýdicé! Eurýdicé!' "

Haec Proteus, et se iactu dedit aequor in altum,
quaque dedit, spumantem undam sub vertice torsit.
at non Cyrene, namque ultro adfata timentem:
"nate, licet tristis animo deponere curas.
haec omnis morbi causa, hinc miserabile Nymphae,
cum quibus illa choros lucis agitabat in altis,
exitium misere apibus. tu munera supplex
tende petens pacem, et facilis venerare Napaeas;
namque dabunt veniam votis, irasque remittent.
sed modus orandi qui sit prius ordine dicam.
quattuor eximios praestanti corpore tauros,
qui tibi nunc viridis depascunt summa Lycaei,
delige et intacta totidem cervice iuvencas.
quattuor his aras alta ad delubra dearum
constitue, et sacrum iugulis demitte cruorem
corporaque ipsa boum frondoso desere luco.
post ubi nona suos Aurora ostenderit ortus,
inferias Orphei Lethaea papavera mittes,
et nigram mactabis ovem, lucumque revises:
placatam Eurydicen vitula venerabere caesa."
    Haud mora: continuo matris praecepta facessit;
ad delubra venit, monstratas excitat aras,
quattuor eximios praestanti corpore tauros
ducit et intacta totidem cervice iuvencas.
post ubi nona suos Aurora induxerat ortus,
inferias Orphei mittit, lucumque revisit.

Thus Proteus, and suddenly he dived
Into the sea; the foaming water swirled
And eddied where he'd dived and disappeared;
The young man was amazed, but the nymph Cyréné
Spoke to him with authority and said,
"My son, it is permitted now for you
To put aside the cares that have disturbed you.
The cause of the sickness has been explained by this:
The Nymphs, with whom Eurýdicé used to dance
In the deep woodland groves, have punished you
By bringing down disaster on your bees.
You must offer gifts to the Nymphs, asking for pardon.
The gentle Nymphs will respond to your supplication;
Their anger will abate; they will forgive you.
But I must tell you how to go about it,
The manner and the order of your rites.
Choose four outstanding bulls, surpassing all
For beauty of conformation, from among
Your herds that graze the slopes of Mount Lycáeus,
And choose four heifers, too, as yet unyoked;
Erect four altars before the goddesses' shrines;
Drain from the victims' throats their sacral blood,
But leave their bodies there in the leafy grove.
After nine dawns of Aurora's rising light,
Then you must make funereal offerings
Of black Lethean poppies to Orpheus,
Slay a black ewe, and then return to the grove."

He followed at once the commandments of his mother:
He went to the sacred place and raised four altars;
He brought four bulls whose beauty surpassed the beauty
Of all the others in the grazing herds;
Four heifers, too, as yet too young for the yoke.
After nine dawns of Aurora's rising light,
He offered to Orpheus black Lethean poppies,
And then he returned to the leafy grove.

hic vero subitum ac dictu mirabile monstrum
aspiciunt, liquefacta boum per viscera toto
stridere apes utero et ruptis effervere costis,
immensasque trahi nubes, iamque arbore summa
confluere et lentis uvam demittere ramis.

Haec super arvorum cultu pecorumque canebam
et super arboribus, Caesar dum magnus ad altum
fulminat Euphraten bello victorque volentis
per populos dat iura viamque adfectat Olympo.
illo Vergilium me tempore dulcis alebat
Parthenope, studiis florentem ignobilis oti,
carmina qui lusi pastorum audaxque iuventa,
Tityre, te patulae cecini sub tegmine fagi.

But there was a sudden, a marvelous event,
A prodigy, miraculous to tell—
Everywhere in the bellies of the victims
Bees buzzing in the fermenting viscera
And bursting forth from the ruptured sides in swarms
That drift along like enormous clouds in the sky
And come together high in the top of a tree
And hang in clusters from the swaying branches.

This song I sang, having sung about the care
Of fields, and trees, and animals, while Caesar
By the deep Euphrates River thundered in war
And gave a conqueror's laws to grateful nations
And gloriously sought Olympian heights,
And I, the poet Virgil, nurtured by sweet
Parthénopé, was flourishing in the pleasures
Of idle studies, I, who bold in youth
Played games with shepherds' songs and, Tityrus, sang
Of how you lay in ease in the beech tree's shade.

NOTES

GLOSSARY

Notes

The title *Georgica* derives from Greek words for farmer, agriculture, working in the earth (*geo*, earth, and *ergon*, work).

INTRODUCTION

xv   "All the blood shed that to this day's unpaid for": Horace, Ode ii.1, in *The Odes of Horace*, trans. David Ferry (New York: Farrar, Straus and Giroux, 1997), p. 203.

xviii   "In and Outdoor Schooling": *Robert Frost: Lectures on the Centennial of His Birth* (Washington, D.C.: Library of Congress, 1975).

FIRST GEORGIC

3   "What's right for bringing abundance to the fields . . . here begins my song": In these opening lines Virgil lists the governing topics of the four Georgics: the cultivation of field crops in the first; the cultivation of vines and fruit trees in the second; the breeding and care of animals in the third; the keeping of bees in the fourth. In the proem or introductory passage he goes on to address his patron Maecenas, and, in prayer, the sponsoring gods of the poem, and finally the ruling prince, Octavian (later to be called Augustus).

3   "the nickering steed was born": Neptune was god of horses, and their first ancestor.

3   "guardian of the groves": Aristaeus, demigod patron of farming, forestry, and beekeeping (see the Fourth Georgic). He was also a herdsman and patron of herdsmen, and in that capacity was called to help the herdsmen on the island of Ceos.

5   "And you, O Caesar": The ruler Octavian, at the time of the writing of this poem not yet called Augustus.

5   "of Venus your goddess mother": Virgil is associating Octavian here with Aeneas, whose father was Priam, his mother Venus; and descent from her is claimed for the Caesars as well.

5   "Proserpina . . . Was reluctant": Because she was Queen of the Under-

world; and of course, when one is anxious for the end of winter, spring seems reluctant.

11 "For Father Jupiter himself ordained": Jupiter (in Greek, Zeus) and his brothers overthrew Saturn (in Greek, Kronos), and thus the Golden Age, when there was no labor, was ended. The passage that begins with these lines is perhaps the most important in the poem, establishing its context and thematic matrix.

13 "oracle of Zeus": Virgil is referring to Dodona, in Greece, where the oldest oracle of the chief god was located.

15 "Darnel and tares and sterile oat-grass thrive": *infelix lolium et steriles dominantur avenae*, almost an exact quotation of line 37 (*infelix lolium et steriles nascuntur avenae*) of Virgil's Fifth Eclogue, where the death of the shepherd Daphnis and its dire consequences for nature are described.

15 "You'll shake the oak tree": In the Saturnian Age, when men didn't need to labor, they subsisted on acorns; here the lazy farmer will have to find acorns to eat.

33 "halcyon birds": Mythical birds supposed to have the power to calm the waters of the sea.

39 "When Caesar's light was quenched": This refers to the assassination of Julius Caesar, and the civil strife that ensued.

41 "this young prince": Octavian, who later became Augustus Caesar.

41 "Priam's father's broken promise at Troy": Laomedon, king of Troy, was said to have broken his promise to pay Apollo and Poseidon for helping to build the walls of the city, and this was seen as the original cause of Troy's disasters and of the civil wars of Rome.

SECOND GEORGIC

47 "Jupiter's grove": At Dodona, the oldest oracle of Zeus, in Greece.

49 "Maecénas . . . Come, spread sail, make haste across the sea": The whole poem is dedicated to Virgil's great patron, and in describing here the great work he is undertaking, Virgil is self-celebrating the grandeur and adventurousness of his task as a heroic sea voyage, and defining the task in more modest terms, at sea but staying close in to shore.

51 "Whose leaves Hercules plucked to make his crown": The myth is that when Hercules brought the hell-dog Cerberus up from Hades, he, Hercules, made himself a crown from the poplar, a tree that grew down there.

51 "born to know the dangers of the seas": That is to say, the wood of the fir tree was used in shipbuilding.

57 "wool-bearing tree": The cotton plant.

57 "silk tree": Some ancient writers thought silk was obtained by combing the leaves of such a tree.

57 "bulls with nostrils breathing fire": Like those in Apollonius's *Argonau-*

tica, tamed by Jason. The lines that immediately follow are also about that episode in Apollonius.

59 Marsians, Sabines, etc.: A catalogue of Italian tribes who became incorporated into the Roman nation.

61 "Victor in Asia": Octavian, triumphant over Antony and Cleopatra.

61 "cowardly Indian": Cleopatra, who committed suicide after having been defeated by Octavian at Actium.

61 "Hesiod's song": The lines here compare Virgil's project in the *Georgics* to that of the early Greek poet Hesiod, in his poem about agricultural life and work, the *Works and Days.*

61 "Minerva's grove": Minerva (Athena) was the patroness of the olive.

63 "elegant Etruscan": Evidently there were Etruscan specialists in ritual musical performances.

63 "unfortunate Mantua": Mantua is the town near Virgil's father's farm, from which he was said to have been dispossessed when Octavian resettled his soldiers after his victory at Philippi.

63 "angry plowman": This passage foreshadows the description of the *bugonia,* Aristaeus's slaughtering of bullocks in order to engender a new stock of bees, and also the comparison of Orpheus's lament, after the second loss of Eurydice, to the sorrowing of a nightingale after "a herdsman, hard of heart," had stolen her young ones from her nest.

71 "Enveloped in the darkness of its leaves": This line of my translation is adapted from Wordsworth's lines about a great ancient yew tree in his poem "Yew-Trees": "There is a Yew-tree, pride of Lorton Vale, / Which to this day stands single, in the midst / Of its own darkness, as it stood of yore . . ." I believe his line also derives from the lines in this Georgic, *tum fortis late ramos et bracchia tendens / huc illuc, media ipsa ingentem sustinet umbram.*

73 "father god": Jupiter, as Jupiter Pluvius, bringer of rain.

79 "curved Saturnian blade": Saturnian perhaps because it resembles the sickle with which Saturn castrated his father, Uranus.

89 "Born on the Cretan mountain": Jupiter, said to have been born on the island of Crete.

THIRD GEORGIC

93 The Third Georgic, like the Fourth, opens with a long proem, this one describing an imaginary temple that Virgil's poetry will build in honor of the ruler Octavian, who will be seated at the center of the temple. The proem looks forward, probably, to the great post-*Georgics* work Virgil is contemplating, the *Aeneid.*

93 "I'll bring the Idumaean palms to you": The palm signifies victory. Virgil is boasting that in his projected poem celebrating Caesar, he'll produce Roman equivalents for foreign heroic celebratory modes.

93   "Molorchus's grove": The site of the Nemean Games, in Greece.

113 "And what about the youth": The youth here is Leander, who swam the Hellespont every night, in order to make love to the beautiful maiden Hero, until one night he drowned.

123 "O Moon": Virgil is referring to a tale, obscure in origin, that the god Pan turned himself into a ram to seduce Luna, the moon; or that he did so by offering her a beautiful fleece.

FOURTH GEORGIC

161 "the spider that Minerva hates": Arachne was a wonderful weaver who challenged Minerva to a weaving duel. Minerva tore the cloth Arachne wove, and Arachne committed suicide and was changed into a spider.

163 "the Arcadian master": Aristaeus (see Glossary).

163 "that flows / Downhill from the swarthy Indians' country": The source of the Nile was disputed, and the poem chooses to believe that Africa and India were one.

167 Drymo, etc.: The names of these nymphs are not further specified in the Glossary, since the passage seems clear without such specification.

169 "the Po, the bellowing bull": The river Eridanus was identified with the Po, and the river is described as a bull because of its roaring waters.

171 Proteus: A sea god, son of Ocean and Tethys.

185 "I . . . nurtured by sweet / Parthénopé": That is, by Naples. The Siren Parthenope was said to have been buried near Naples. Virgil lived in a villa near that city.

185 "Played games with shepherds' songs": Virgil is referring to the *Eclogues*, his earlier work, and the last line of the *Georgics* (*Tityre, te patulae cecini sub tegmine fagi*) is almost identical with the first line of the First Eclogue, (*Tityre, tu patulae recubans sub tegmine fagi*).

Glossary

ABYDOS: A town on the Asian side of the Hellespont, at its narrowest point.

ACERRAE: A deserted town in the Campania, not far from Rome. Deserted perhaps because of a flooding of the river Clanius, or for other reasons (perhaps a massacre, perhaps malaria).

ACHELOUS: A river in Greece.

ACHERON: One of the five rivers of Hades.

ACHILLES: The greatest warrior of the Greeks, in the Trojan War; son of Peleus and the sea goddess Thetis.

ACROCERAUNIA: A mountainous headland in what is now Albania; "the Thunder Mountain."

AETNA: A volcanic mountain in Sicily.

ALBURNUS: A mountain in southern Italy, near Paestum.

ALCINOUS: King of the Phaeacians.

ALPHEUS: A river god who pursued the nymph Arethusa to Sicily, where she became a fountain.

AMINNAEAN: A kind of wine; also another name for myrrh.

AMPHRYSOS: A river in Thessaly, associated with Apollo.

AMYTHAON: The father of the soothsayer Melampus.

ANIO: A tributary of the Tiber, Rome's river.

AONIAN MOUNTAIN: Boeotia, the part of the Greek mainland where Mount Helicon is.

APOLLO: The son of Zeus and Latona, brother of Diana. Born on the island of Delos. The sun god and god of the arts.

AQUARIUS: "The Water Carrier." A constellation and one of the signs of the zodiac.

AQUILO: The North Wind.

ARCADIA: A region of the Peloponnese in Greece; the native region of the god Pan; the home country of pastoral song.

ARCTOS: Constellation, the "Little Bear." Jupiter had turned his father, the Arcadian king Lycaon, into a wolf, and his mother into "the Great Bear."

ARCTURUS: A star in the constellation Boötes.

ARETHUSA: A wood nymph who was pursued by the river god Alpheus. She fled from him and was turned into a fountain in Sicily.

ARGITIS: A wine made from white grapes.

ARGOS: A giant with a hundred eyes.

ARIADNE: The daughter of Minos of Crete. She helped Theseus kill the Minotaur and to escape from Crete. They were married but Theseus deserted her. She later married Bacchus. She became a constellation.

ARISTAEUS: The son of Apollo and the sea nymph Cyrene. He was a farmer and a patron of the skills of farming; he was also a beekeeper. He caused the first death of Eurydice by attempting to rape her, pursuing her along a riverbank where she was fatally bitten by a serpent. He learned the art of *bugonia*, by which bees were engendered in the bellies of slaughtered cattle.

ASCANIUS: A river in Asia Minor.

ASSARACUS: The father of Anchises, who was, with Venus, a parent of Aeneas.

ASSYRIA: A Mesopotamian kingdom.

ATHENA: The Greek goddess of wisdom; Minerva was her Roman name.

ATHOS: A mountain in northeastern Greece.

ATTICA: The region of Greece where Athens is located.

AURORA: The goddess of the dawn.

AUSTER: The South Wind.

AVERNUS, LAKE: A lake near Naples, thought to be the entrance to the Underworld.

BACCHANTES: Female followers and priestesses of Bacchus.

BACCHUS: The Roman name for Dionysus, god of wine, festivity, inspiration, and, in some contexts, moderation.

BACTRIA: A region north of what is now Iran.

BALEARIC: Islands in the Mediterranean Sea (Majorca and Minorca).

BEARS, THE: Two constellations, Ursa Major and Ursa Minor. They are always visible in the nighttime sky, never sinking below the horizon.

BENACUS, LAKE: A lake near Verona, now called the Lago di Gardia.

BOÖTES: A constellation.

BOREAS: The North Wind (also called Aquilo).

BUSIRIS: An Egyptian king killed by Hercules. He practiced human sacrifice.

CAICUS: A river in Asia Minor.

CALABRIA: Now the name for the "toe" of Italy, the southwestern extremity; in ancient days it referred to the "heel," the southeastern extremity.

CANIS: The Dog Star constellation.

CANOPIA: A town and island at the western mouth of the Nile.

CAPUA: The principal Campanian town, east of Rome.

CARPATHIANS: A range of mountains in central Europe.

CASTALIA: A nymph, pursued by Apollo, who became a spring on Mount Parnassus.

CAUCASUS: A mountain range in Asia.

CAURUS: The Northwest Wind.

CEAEAN: Of the Cycladic island Ceos, associated with Aristaeus's farming and beekeeping.

CELEUS: King of Eleusis. He was a source of agricultural wisdom who helped Ceres find Persephone.

CENTAURS: Half-horse, half-man, they lived in Thessaly, north of Greece.

CERBERUS: The three-headed (or many-headed) guardian dog of Hades.

CERES: The goddess of agriculture, mother of Proserpina (Persephone).

CHALYBIA: A region on the south shore of the Black Sea.

CHAONIAN: Of a region in northwestern Greece.

CHIOS: An island in the Aegean Sea.

CHIRON: The wisest of the Centaurs.

CICONIA: A region of southern Thrace.

CILICIA: Region, and Roman province, of Asia Minor.

CITHAERON: A mountain range in northern Greece.

CLANIUS: A river in the Campania whose flooding may have caused the depopulation of the town of Acerrae.

CLITUMNUS: An Umbrian river. The legend was that cattle that drank from it turned white as snow.

COCYTOS: One of the five rivers of Hades.

COEUS: One of the Titans, children of Uranus, the sky god, oldest of the gods, and Gaea, the earth goddess.

CORYBANTES: The Curetes, priests of Cybele.

CORYCIA: A region of Asia Minor.

CRETAN: Of the island of Crete.

CRUSTUMIAN: Of a tribe near Rome.

CURETES: The Corybantes, priests of the goddess Cybele.

CYBELE: A fertility goddess, the "Magna Mater," sometimes associated with Ceres. The ritual dances in honor of her were accompanied by the sound of cymbals.

CYCLOPS: One-eyed cannibal sons of Poseidon (Neptune), the god of the sea. Their cave was at the foot of Mount Aetna in Sicily.

CYLLARUS: A horse given by Neptune to Juno, who then gave it to Pollux.

CYNTHIAN: A mountain on the island of Delos, Apollo's birthplace.

CYPRUS: A great island in the eastern Mediterranean.

CYRENE: A nymph who was the mother of Aristaeus; his father was Apollo.

CYTORUS, MOUNT: A mountain in Asia Minor.

DACIANS: A people living north of the Danube, in Transylvania.

DELOS: An Aegean island, birthplace of Apollo.

DEUCALION: The Greek and Roman Noah. After the great Flood, he and his wife, Pyrrha, restarted the human race, he by throwing stones which became men, she by throwing stones which became women.

DICTE: The cave where Zeus (Jupiter) was born and hidden from his father Kronos, who would have eaten him. Virgil is saying in these lines that Zeus rewarded the bees for feeding him on honey when he was a baby.

DRYADS: Wood nymphs.

ELEUSIS: A rich Greek city, in Attica but independent of Athens. Site of the agricultural "mysteries," ceremonies worshipping Demeter and Persephone.

ELYSIAN FIELDS: Home of the blessed, in the afterlife.

EMATHIA: A region of Macedonia, where Caesar defeated Pompey in 48 B.C.E.

ENIPEUS: A river in Thessaly.

EPHYRAEUS: The old name for Corinth, a Greek city famous for its bronzes.

EPIDAURUS: A Greek city in the northwestern Peloponnese.

EPIRUS: A region in northwestern Greece.

EREBUS: A passage in the Underworld.

ERICHTHONIUS: King of Athens, favorite of Athena; he invented chariot driving.

ETRURIA: An ancient region of western Italy, along the Tyrrhenian Sea.

EUMENIDES: The Furies.

EUPHRATES: One of the great rivers of Mesopotamia.

EURYDICE: The wife of Orpheus.

EURYSTHEUS: King of Argos, who commanded Hercules to perform the Twelve Labors.

FALERNIAN: A famous Roman wine, from the Campania, near Rome.

FAUNS: Goat-legged rural deities.

GALAESUS: A river in Apulia, near Tarentum.

GANGARIDES: A people living on the banks of the Ganges River.

GARGARA: A rich region in Asia Minor.

GELONIANS: A people living in Scythia.

GETAE: A Thracian people, on the lower Danube.

GIANTS: Sons of Uranus, the sky god, and Gaea, the earth goddess. The Giants rebelled unsuccessfully against the gods.

GLAUCUS: Aphrodite caused his racing mares to tear him to pieces because he kept them from breeding. Another Glaucus was a fisherman who became a sea deity.

GOATS, THE: A constellation, the Kids.

HADES: One of the names of the king of the Underworld; a name for the Underworld.

HAEMUS: Haemus and Rhodope were so happy that they took the names of Zeus and Hera, and Zeus turned them into mountains near Philippi, where Octavian and Antony defeated Brutus and the other assassins of Julius Caesar.

HEBRUS: A river in Thrace, in northern Greece.

HELICON: A mountain in Greece, site of a temple of Apollo and the Muses.

HELLESPONT: The strait between the Black Sea and the Sea of Marmara and the Mediterranean.

HERCULES: The Roman name for Heracles, son of Zeus and the mortal Alcmene. Famous for his strength.

HERMUS: A large river in Asia Minor.

HIPPODAMIA: Wife of Pelops and mother of Thyestes and Atreus.

HYADES: Group of stars rising in the rainy season.

HYDASPES: The Hydaspes was a river in India, a tributary of the Indus.

HYLAS: A beautiful boy taken on the *Argo* by Heracles. He went ashore seeking water and was abducted by enamored nymphs. Heracles abandoned the voyage to search for him.

HYPANIS: A river in Scythia; one of the dividers of Europe and Asia.

HYPERBOREANS: A fabled people living in the Far North.

IACCHUS: A minor deity sometimes associated with the Eleusinian Mysteries and with Bacchus or Dionysus.

IAPETUS: A Titan, a son of Earth and Heaven; the father of Prometheus and Atlas.

IDA: A nymph; also a wooded range of mountains in Asia Minor named after her; also a mountain in Crete associated with the youth of Zeus.

IDUMAEA: A region in Palestine.

ILLYRIA: A region in western Greece.

INACHUS: Io's father.

IO: Zeus changed her into a heifer to hide her from Hera. She fled to Egypt, tormented by a gadfly. Zeus turned her back into a woman.

IONIAN: The eastern coastal region of the Adriatic Sea.

ISMARA, MOUNT: A mountain in Thrace, north of Greece.

IXION: King of Thessaly, legendary killer, "the Greek Cain"; he tried to seduce Hera, Zeus's wife; he fathered the Centaurs on a cloud disguised as Hera. Zeus had him tied everlastingly to a turning wheel in Hades.

JOVE: Another name for Jupiter, the Roman Zeus, the chief of the gods.

JUNO: The Roman name for Hera; the wife of Jupiter.

JUPITER: The Roman Zeus, the chief of the gods.

KIDS, THE: A constellation, the Goats.

LAGEAN: Egyptian.

LAPITHS: A Thessalian people, enemies of the Centaurs, whom they fought at the wedding banquet of their king, Pirithous.

LARIUS, LAKE: A lake in northern Italy, now called Lago di Como.

LATONA: The mother of Apollo and Diana.

LESBOS: An Aegean island, birthplace of the poets Sappho and Alcaeus.

LETHE: The river of oblivion, in the Underworld.

LIBER: An Italian fertility god, god of wine and festivity, identified in the poem with Bacchus.

LIBYA: A region of North Africa.

LUCIFER: A name for the morning star.

LUCRINUS, LAKE: A lagoon near Naples. Agrippa enlarged it as an anchorage by linking it to Lake Avernus.

LUNA: The moon.

LYCAEUS, MOUNT: An Arcadian mountain where Zeus was born; associated with the god Pan.

LYCAON: An Arcadian king, turned by Jupiter into a wolf.

LYCUS: A river flowing into the Black Sea, as does the river Phasis.

LYDIA: A country in Asia Minor.

MACEDONIA: A region north of Greece.

MAECENAS: The patron of Virgil and Horace. A senior adviser to Augustus.

MAENALUS: A mountain sacred to Pan, in Arcadia.

MAEONIA: One of the places where Homer was supposed to have been born.

MAIA: One of the Pleiades; mother of Mercury; the month of May.

MANES, THE: Spirits of the dead.

MANTUA: A town in northern Italy; Virgil was born nearby.

MAREOTIS, LAKE: A lake in Egypt, near Alexandria.

MARS: The god of war.

MASSIC: Wine grown on the slopes of Mount Massicus, in the Apennines.

MEDEA: A sorceress who married Jason of the Argonauts, who deserted her; she killed her children, and later became a queen of Athens.

MEDES: A people of a region called Media, in what is now Iran.

MELAMPUS: A soothsayer.

MELICERTA: He and his mother leaped into the sea when his father threatened to kill them. They were turned into sea deities.

MELLA: A tributary of the river Po. "Mella" means "honey."

MERCURY: The Roman name of Hermes, messenger of the gods, god of commerce, eloquence, thievery; inventor of the lyre.

MILETIAN: Of Miletus, a maritime power in the eastern Mediterranean; famous for its textiles and furniture.

MINCIUS: A river that flows past Mantua in northern Italy.

MINERVA: The Roman Athena, goddess of wisdom.

MOLORCHUS: A shepherd. Hercules killed the Nemean lion, which had killed Molorchus's son. The Nemean Games were played in a grove Molorchus had planted.

MOLOSSIANS: A tribe in western Greece that supported the Macedonians against the Romans and were destroyed as a power in 167 B.C.E.

MYCENAE: An ancient town in the Peloponnese.

MYSIA: A region in northwestern Asia Minor.

NARYCUM: A town in Greece.

NEREIDS: Sea nymphs.

NEREUS: Sea god, son of Oceanus and Gaea, the earth mother.

NIPHATES: A people of a mountainous region of Armenia.

NISUS: King of Megara, whose daughter, Scylla, cut off a purple lock of his hair that his throne depended on; she offered it to Minos, king of Crete, in order to woo him. He accepted it, but not her, and she committed suicide. She was turned into a lark, and her father into a hawk.

NORICAN: Of the region now called Austria.

NYMPHS: Lesser divinities, maidens attendant on the gods.

OLYMPIA: Town in the northwestern Peloponnese, where the first Olympic Games were held. Site of a famous temple to Zeus.

OLYMPUS, MOUNT: The highest mountain in Greece, home of the gods.

ORCUS: God of the Underworld; therefore, often a name for the Underworld.

ORITHYIA: Daughter of a king of Athens. She was carried off by the North Wind and became his wife.

ORPHEUS: Son of Apollo and the Muse Calliope. The greatest of singers and musicians, playing the lyre Apollo had given him. When Eurydice died, his music persuaded the gods of the Underworld to permit him to bring her back to life as long as he did not turn to look at her on the journey back. Virgil may have invented in this poem Orpheus's turning back to look at her, thus losing her forever.

OSSA, MOUNT: A mountain in Thessaly.

PAESTUM: A town in southern Italy, famous for its roses and for the temples built there when it was a Greek colony.

PALATINE: The most important of the seven hills of Rome.

PALES: Goddess of cattle and pastures.

PALLENE: A peninsula in Asia Minor, across the Aegean Sea from Thessaly.

PAN: The Arcadian god of flocks, shepherds, farming, and woodlands; half goat, half man; a son of Hermes.

PANCHAEAN: Arabian.

PANGAEA: A mountain in Macedonia.

PANOPEA: A sea nymph, one of the Nereids.

PARIAN: Of the island of Paros, famous for its marble.

PARNASSUS: A sacred mountain in Greece, site of the Delphic oracle.

PARTHENOPE: A sea nymph, one of the three Sirens, a daughter of Calliope. She was said to be buried near Naples.

PARTHIA: A country in western Asia, now Iran.

PELETHRONIUS: The region of the Lapiths and Centaurs, in Thessaly.

PELION: A mountain in Thessaly. In the war against the gods, the Giants piled Mount Ossa on top of it, trying to reach the gods. Centaurs lived on the mountain.

PELOPS: Zeus's grandchild, Tantalus's son; husband of Hippodamia, whom he won in a horse race; father of Atreus and Thyestes, and grandfather of Agamemnon and Menelaus. Killed and cooked by his father, and served to the gods. Demeter ate his shoulder, and when Zeus restored Pelops to life, he had an ivory shoulder.

PENEUS: A river god; the river named for him.

PHAEACIA: An island in the Ionian Sea; Odysseus was shipwrecked there.

PHANAE: A town on the Aegean island of Chios.

PHASIS: A river flowing into the Black Sea, as does the river Lycus.

PHILIPPI: A Macedonian town where Brutus and other assassins of Caesar were defeated by Octavian and Antony.

PHILLYRA: Parent of the wise Centaur Chiron, famous for his medical knowledge.

PHRYGIA: A region of western Asia Minor; the country of Troy.

PISCES: "The Fish," a constellation and a sign of the zodiac.

PLEIADES: A constellation, associated with rainy weather.

PLUVIUS: Jupiter as rain bringer.

PO: A great river in northern Italy.

POLLUX: Twin brother of Castor; their constellation, Gemini, heralds and fosters calm weather at sea.

PONTUS: The Black Sea.

POTNIA: A place in Greece near Thebes.

PRECIAN: A kind of grapevine.

PRIAM: King of Troy when Troy fell.

PRIAPUS: The god of procreation; his ithyphallic statue was put up in gardens to ward off thieves. There was a worship site to Priapus at Lampsacus, on the banks of the Hellespont.

PROCNE: Her husband, Tereus, king of Thrace, raped her sister Philomela, and cut out Philomela's tongue. Procne and Philomela cooked and served Itylus, Procne and Tereus's little son, to Tereus in revenge. Philomela was turned by the gods into a nightingale, Procne into a swallow, Tereus into a hawk, and Itylus into a sandpiper.

PROSERPINA: The Latin name of Persephone, daughter of Ceres; carried off by Hades to become queen of the Underworld; returns to the upper world each spring.

PROTEUS: "The old man," a sea god, son of Ocean and Tethys.

PSITHIAN: A variety of wine grape.

QUIRINUS: The name of an ancient Roman tribe; a martial god worshipped on the Quirinal Hill in Rome, this god is identified with the deified Romulus, founder of Rome.

RHAETIA: A Roman province in the Alps.

RHODES: A great island in the Mediterranean.

RHODOPE: A mountain range in Thrace.

RIPHAEUS: A fabled northern mountain range.

ROMULUS AND REMUS: The twin founders of Rome.

ROSTRUM: A speaker's platform in the Roman Forum.

SABAEANS: An Arabian people.

SABELLI: A general name for the various people who inhabited regions near Rome.

SABINES: An Italian people living in a region near Rome.

SATURN: The Roman equivalent of Kronos, father of the gods, who overthrew him. The planet Saturn. The Age of Saturn was the Golden Age.

SCYLLA: This Scylla (not the sea monster) was the daughter of the king of Megara. To win the love of Minos, king of Crete, she cut off a lock of her sleeping father's purple hair. Minos accepted the power this gave him and conquered Megara, but he refused to marry Scylla, who committed suicide and was turned into a lark, perpetually pursued by the hawk her father had been turned into.

SCYTHIA: A vast region north of the Black Sea.

SERES: The Chinese.

SILA: A wooded mountain range in southern Italy.

SILARUS: A river in southern Italy.

SISYPHUS: "The craftiest of men," as Homer described him. He was the son-in-law of Atlas. He raped Anticlea, the wife of Laertes, and she bore Odysseus. He was the father, by the wife of his brother, of many children, but she killed them all. For these crimes and for insults to the gods, Zeus punished him by giving him the eternal task of rolling a huge stone uphill, over and over, because it immediately rolled back down again.

SNAKE: A constellation.

SPARTA: A city in the Peloponnese.

SPERCHEUS: A river in Thessaly.

STRYMON: A river in Thrace and Macedonia.

STYGIUS: A name for the Underworld, the place of the river Styx.

STYX: The principal river of the Underworld; also a name for the Underworld.

SYLVANUS: Italian god of uncultivated land, half goat, half man; often identified with Faunus or Pan.

TABURNUS: A mountain in the Apennine range in central Italy.

TAENARUS: A cape in the southernmost Peloponnese, where there was a cavern supposed to be an entrance to the Underworld.

TANAGER: A river in southern Italy.

TARENTUM: A city in the heel of southern Italy.

TARTARUS: The lowest region of the Underworld.

TAURUS: A mountain range in Asia Minor; a constellation, the second sign of the zodiac.

TAYGETA: A mountain range in Laconia (Sparta) in the Peloponnese.

TAYGETE: A star in the constellation Pleiades.

TEMPE: A beautiful valley in Thessaly.

TETHYS: Ocean's sister and wife; daughter of Earth and Heaven; mother of all the rivers.

THASOS: An island in the Aegean, off the coast of Thrace.

THESSALY: A region north of Greece.

THETIS: A sea deity, wife of the Thessalian king Peleus. Her son was Achilles.

THRACE: A region north of Greece.

THYMBRA: The site of an oracle of Apollo, on the island of Crete.

TIMAVUS: A river in northeastern Italy, near what is now Trieste.

TIMOLUS: King of Lydia, in Asia Minor; the name of a Lydian mountain.

TISIPHONE: One of the Furies.

TITHONUS: Brother of Priam, king of Troy. He was so beautiful that Aurora fell in love with him and made him immortal. But he was not impervious to the effects of aging. He could not die, but he could grow old. Finally he was turned into a grasshopper.

TRIPTOLEMUS: The goddess Demeter loved him. He learned the arts of agriculture from her, and taught them to men.

TROS: Grandson of the founder of Troy, Dardanus.

TROY: Ancestral city of Rome, in Asia Minor. Aeneas, founder of Rome, came to Italy after the fall of Troy to the Greeks.

TYPHOEUS: A huge monster buried by Zeus (Jupiter) under Mount Aetna.

TYRE: A city on the eastern coast of the Mediterranean. It was famous for its purple dye.

ULTIMA THULE: An island in the North Sea, the end of the world to the north.

VENUS: The Roman name of Aphrodite, goddess of love.

VESPER: The evening star.

VESTA: Goddess of the hearth, protectress of Rome.

VESUVIUS: A volcano near Naples.

VIRGIN: A constellation; the sixth sign of the zodiac.

WAGON, THE: A constellation, the Big Dipper.

ZEPHYR: A West Wind.

ZEUS: The Greek name of Jupiter or Jove, the god of heaven and earth.